WISDOM OF THE AGES

Extraordinary People 19 to 90

Edited by PATRICIA M. HINDS

Introduction by SUSAN L. TAYLOR

ESSENCE
BOOKS

Time Inc. Home Entertainment

President: Rob Gursha
Vice-president, Branded Businesses: David Arfine
Vice-president, New Product Development: Richard Fraiman
Executive Director, Marketing Services: Carol Pittard
Director, Retail & Special Sales: Tom Mifsud
Director of Finance: Tricia Griffin
Associate Director, New Product Development: Peter Harper
Prepress Manager: Emily Rabin
Associate Book Production Manager: Suzanne Janso

Special thanks: Bozena Bannett, Gina Di Meglio, Robert Dente, Anne-Michelle Gallero, Natalie McCrea, Robert Marasco, Jonathan Polsky, Mary Jane Rigoroso, Steven Sandonato, Grace Sullivan

ISBN: 1-932273-16-6

We welcome your comments and suggestions about Essence Books. Please write to us at:
Essence Books
Attention: Book Editors
P.O. Box 11016
Des Moines, IA 50336–1016

If you would like to order any of our hardcover Collector's Edition books, please call us at 1-800-327-6388
(Monday through Friday, 7:00 A.M.–8:00 P.M. or Saturday, 7:00 A.M.–6:00 P.M. Central Time).

CONTRIBUTORS

Editor-in-Chief: Patricia M. Hinds
Writers: Joy Duckett Cain, Deborah Gregory, Diane Patrick
Contributing Editor: Rosemarie Robotham
Editorial Assistants: Janell Hazelwood, Niani Taylor
Copy Editors: Maxine Bartow, Sherrill Clarke, Hope Wright
Designer/Art Director: Eve Sandler
Design/Production Assistant: Nicole Alleyne
Interviewers: Cassidy Arkin, Jenyne Raines
Photo Researcher: Danielle Collins
Administrative Assistants: Michael Morgan, Starrene Rhett

Produced and packaged by Mignon Communications

Special thanks: Diane Weathers, Marlowe Goodson, Jan deChabert, LaVon Leak-Wilks, Sandra Martin, Cheryl Fenton, asha bandele, Sharon Boone, Karen Brown, Denolyn Carroll, Faith Childs-Davis, Monique Davis, Alison France, Abdullah Hassan, Tamara Jeffries, Marsha Kelly, Claire McIntosh, Cori M. Murray, Debra Parker, Danielle Robinson, Lena Sherrod, Mikki Taylor, Linda Villarosa, Charlotte Wiggers

Acknowledgments: Gregory Boyea, Jennelle Mahone-Sy, Edgerton Maloney, Paul Nocera, Larry Ramo, Leah Rudolfo, Penny Wrenn

CONTENTS

THE SACRED JOURNEY

I have so loved editing this inspiring and informative book with Patricia Hinds, the editor of Essence's book-publishing division. The extraordinary women and men who share their stories in these pages speak in voices so sure, so strong and so very loving that they will make your heart sing with hope and possibility. They may even change your life. Their stories, and the wisdom and passion for living they have gained on the many roads they've traveled, certainly changed mine. They remind me of what we too often forget: Life is a sacred journey. God did not send any of us here weak or incomplete. Instead, the Creator gave each of us the power to choose our path—again and again. This power to choose is the divine force in each of us, and we must learn to respect and use it continuously to set our course right.

The women and men you will meet here represent every age and stage of life. They are 19 to 90. Some are celebrities, whose names you know and whose work you love. Others are everyday folk, whom you may be learning about for the first time. All are shining examples of the fact that, no matter how off course we may wander, no matter how lost or abandoned we may feel, we still have this amazing power to redirect ourselves, to choose a path to spiritual, mental and physical wellness, every day of our lives.

Many of the individuals included here first shared their experiences in ESSENCE. It was our happy task to revisit these friends, to update their stories and compile them into this one exquisite volume. *Wisdom of the Ages: Extraordinary People 19 to 90* gives us a unique perspective on how to achieve a life of balance and harmony, a life that honors the divine within ourselves. Most important, each person offers practical advice and the personal wisdom that comes from living life courageously, facing down fear and embracing the knowledge that God has given us *everything* we need to overcome any challenge.

Through my own life and through the lives of the many people I've been privileged to know in my three decades at ESSENCE, I have come to realize that it's the rare soul among us who does not actually fall down first. Indeed, our trials serve us in wonderful and unexpected ways. We need not fear physical illness or emotional pain. We need not fear any of the challenges life sends our way, because they help us generate the will, the energy and the fortitude necessary to propel ourselves to the next level, to reach higher than we might ever otherwise dream. This volume bears witness to the fact that any fall is always in divine order, life is always on our side, and God always has our back.

"It is the Creator's intention that we live peacefully, patiently, healthfully and joyfully, and we should accept nothing less."

In many ways this is a book about the power of commitment. It is about women and men who have chosen to simplify their lives by choosing healthy, holistic ways of being in the world. Some have made dietary changes. Some, even in their 70s and 80s, have adopted fitness routines that have restored their youthfulness and vitality. Some describe letting go of toxic relationships, reducing stress, overcoming a health crisis or pausing to appreciate the patient devotion of loved ones. Still others have had the challenge of learning to love and cherish themselves and the gift of their lives in order to break through emotional barriers. Each person's experience so richly illustrates the power of consistency. When we honor the commitment to do whatever is necessary to nourish ourselves and others, the universe opens up to us and pours forth blessings greater than anything we ever imagined.

What I so love about life is that change is always possible. It's never too late. We can always correct our course. This treasury of hard-earned wisdom helps us remember that the only place on earth where infinite growth is possible is within us. Aging is meant to be a magnificent adventure. It is the Creator's intention that we live peacefully, patiently, healthfully and joyfully, and we should accept nothing less. The doorway to a radiant life is always open. There is always a way to heal what ails us, and often, the answers will be found not in a doctor's office, but within ourselves. As the stories in these pages remind us, our lives grow in the direction of our choices, and with each breath we have the power to choose again, to choose consciously and wisely the path that leads to loving and living without limits.

The Essence family offers this book with the hope that it will help open your hearts and minds to your own full measure of joy. It is our wish that the divine right teachers, healers and experiences will flow into our lives so that we may bring the healing that is so needed to our people.

SUSAN L. TAYLOR

9

"*Real luxury is about just being able to be with the people you love.*"

— COMMON

LIVING
IN LOVE

BEYONCÉ

Singer and actress Beyoncé Knowles started singing at age 8 and later performed in the hot group Destiny's Child. She has a great deal of admiration for the women in her life, including her mother—who gave up a successful hair salon to help guide her daughter's career. Beyoncé delights in the love of sisterhood.

Admiring your elders:

"I relate to older Black women. There's always something to learn. I grew up around my mom and her friends in her salon, so I've always been surrounded by phenomenal Black women."

An oasis for sister talk:

"I saw women come in and use the salon as a place for therapy—telling all. People would have a drink, get their hair done and relax. Women can talk for hours and hours. But we can also communicate without talking, because we go through so many of the same things. We feel each other. It's a connection."

Learning by listening:

"There are certain people whose aura is so strong you can see the wisdom. I love to be around women like that. I know there are a lot of things I haven't been through, so I just want to listen to them and soak up as much as I can."

Beloved mother:

"I can be my whole self in front of my mother. She's my friend, and we have a soul connection that is irreplaceable. She has an impact on every female around her."

Family ties:

"My mom is the rock in our family. She didn't take any mess, but she stood by my dad. They had their problems, as in any other marriage, but she protected us and held everything together. Everybody thought my dad was crazy when he left his job to manage us. My mom did, too, but she said, 'I believe in him—I don't understand it, but I'm his wife. I'll work extra hard for my family if I need to.' She was always optimistic. If she didn't make that sacrifice, I wouldn't be where I am today."

Knowles's wisdom:

"Listen to the stories and advice of wise women. What they know and have experienced can save us a lot of heartache."

12

22

Beyoncé with her mother, Tina Knowles.

75

Maya Angelou

Our beloved author, poet, playwright, actress, director and teacher Maya Angelou rose to fame in 1970, with the publication of I Know Why the Caged Bird Sings. *Since then the St. Louis native has inspired us all with her spirit of love and the power of her words, including her sixth autobiographical installment,* A Song Flung From Heaven.

Seventysomething joy:

"I am enjoying myself these days. Actually, I don't know any other way to live. If I wasn't amused, I'd get out of it. That's the way I feel about life. I'm blessed with high energy, and I throw down in all areas."

Being in love:

"I'm in love and have been for many years. And I'm happy to say I'm loved in return. That doesn't always happen. But it's very nice to love someone as your own unmitigated self and hear someone say, 'I also love you.' Someone who keeps a smile on your face. There are those who talk about love. What they really mean is possession. Love liberates; love frees."

Surrounded by love:

"I find comfort in the job that I've done, in friendships, love affairs and business relationships. I'm comforted when young people or older people say that I've been an inspiration."

Pondering pure joy:

"This morning at 6:00, I was thinking about being in Tuscany and sitting in the sun 25 years ago. And then I thought about being in Ghana, in a shower that opened onto the courtyard, where, if no one was there, I could just take off my clothes under that wonderful blue sky. I was thinking about what delicious times I've had and am having, and hope to continue having as long as I'm amused."

Constant creation:

"Not everything you write is going to be a masterpiece. Not everything you cook is great, nor everything you paint—but you're trying for it. When you reach your sixties or seventies or eighties, you won't have to be jealous of young people, because you can say, 'When I was there, I did that thing fully, and now I'm here, doing this thing fully.'"

Angelou's wisdom:

"Live a fulfilling life. Give yourself time just to be with yourself. Don't always try to work out problems when you're alone. Relax. Go for walks. Listen to kids laugh. Breathe deeply and think more profoundly."

BORIS KODJOE

After graduating from Virginia Commonwealth University, where he was enrolled on a tennis scholarship, Boris Kodjoe had a chance encounter with a Ford Modeling Agency scout. Within seven months the Freiberg, Germany, native—who speaks four languages—landed 12 campaigns, including Versace, the Gap and Ralph Lauren. Hollywood took notice, and Kodjoe made his acting debut in the film Love and Basketball, *then landed a feature role on the hit cable television series* Soul Food. *As for love, he knows what he wants in a woman.*

Personal priorities:

"The well-being of my loved ones is number one on my list. And I have learned that I have to love myself to love others."

Biggest turn-on:

"I like ambitious women who have a sense of humor and love kids. It doesn't matter how tall, short, light or dark she is. I like a woman who has calm sophistication and confidence. It lets you know that she is cool with who she is. Being comfortable with yourself is very sexy to me."

A special one:

"I know it's romance when I can't stop smiling, no matter where we are or what we're doing. It's great when we're completely happy and I don't want to be anywhere else—when all I need is that person."

When it's on:

"I really love it when a woman and I reach the point where we have nonverbal communication. I love it when a woman knows what I'm thinking without my saying a word. When it's that strong, it's on!"

Fantasy and reality:

"I love the book *The Little Prince* by Antoine de Saint Exupéry. Every time I read it, I find something new. We are always in search of fulfillment, and our vision of that fulfillment changes as we struggle with life. But in the end, it's still determined by self-love and love of family."

Kodjoe's wisdom:

"I want to teach and be taught about love and communication, the celebration of you and me."

27

ERYKAH BADU & COMMON

Grammy Award winner Erykah Badu and her soul mate, hip-hop artist Common, share more than a love of music. When the pair became romantically involved, each brought a child—as well as emotional baggage—with them from previous relationships. But through their friendship and love, Erykah and Common share a special union.

First impressions:

Common—"I loved Erykah immediately because of how our spirits connected. But the love we shared was more of a brother-sister type of thing."

Erykah—"Our friendship was so important. Here was a man who laughed at my jokes, who enjoyed the food I cooked and who made me feel protected—because he wanted me to be happy."

Challenges faced:

Erykah—"The new Black family includes baby mamas and baby daddies, your spouse, all the children and all the in-laws. We have to accept this and make the best of it."

What it takes to have a healthy relationship:

Erykah—"I see negative feelings—whatever they are, like jealousy—as the opposite of love. I don't want negativity in our lives."

Common—"There's a discipline and a focus you must have if you want to be in a healthy relationship. That, for me, meant letting go of womanizing, drinking and dishonesty."

What they know for sure:

Erykah—"I don't know what the future has for us. Our relationship is much bigger than being boyfriend and girlfriend, husband and wife. We have some very important work to do together as people—in this city, in this country and in this world. The most important part of this union is reconstructing what has been damaged inside and around us."

Common—"We're just striving to do the right thing. We're trying to deal with our imperfections and get to the best place we can. This relationship is sacred to me. This sister was sent to me by God to help me grow. And that, more than anything else, is what I'm going to honor as best I can."

Their wisdom:

Erykah—"My luxury isn't about limousines. It's much more about living someplace where I can leave the door open."

Common—"Real luxury is about just being able to be with the people you love."

44

JERRI DEVARD

Marketing executive Jerri DeVard has been married for 20 years. She and her husband, Gregg, have created a vision for the loving life they want to live and a plan for making that happen.

Key to love:

"I found someone who is my soul mate. In youth we select based on short-term compatibility, but I picked someone who can run the marathon with me — someone with vision and stamina."

Choosing love wisely:

"I saw a person who would not only be a lover but also a partner, a father and a champion. Gregg is a genuine person with high morals, ethics and integrity. Those are endearing traits. Ours is a very healthy and nurturing relationship, and I love him more today than the day I married him."

Quality time:

"We sit down with our daughter and son every night and have dinner. We go around the table, and each person talks about what went on during his or her day. We want to raise our children to be critical thinkers, and we want to probe their minds and find out how they're thinking. We discuss culture and what's going on in the news. We want the children included in everything. When the kids go to bed, my husband and I talk the rest of the night."

Making stress disappear:

"Maybe I'm in denial, but I don't feel stress. To avoid it, I work out with a personal trainer twice a week, and when our family attends church, I use that time to reflect on the many blessings I enjoy."

DeVard's wisdom:

"Know thyself. Know what you enjoy and what you dislike, and choose someone who shares your vision."

BERNIE MAC

Comedian Bernie Mac has won America over as the bumbling father figure on The Bernie Mac Show, *but he is not inept in matters of love. At 19, he married Rhonda, his high school sweetheart, and they have been married for 27 years. As funny as he is onstage, Bernie Mac is dead serious about maintaining that special relationship.*

Being serious about love:

"My wife and I are as tight as a pair of drawers. We met in high school; she was 15 and I was 16. My friend was dating one of her friends, and we all started eating lunch together. We went to the prom, and then we hung out all summer. One night Rhonda and I were sitting on the sofa at her house, and I said, 'I was thinking about permanently hooking up,' and her whole family jumped up out of nowhere!"

Fear of dating again:

"I'm telling you right now, if something were to happen to my marriage, I would not ever date again in my life. I could not sit on someone's couch and get reacquainted."

Working with young beauties:

"When Michael Douglas does a love scene, people say, 'That was a hell of a love scene. I liked the way he showed his feelings.' They don't ask, 'What does his wife think?' To hell with what my wife thinks. I'm a pro."

Funny, but sincere:

"Maybe what I do is funny, but it's from the heart. When I act, I give you my best. I ain't going to cheat you. And I ain't going to cheat in my relationship either."

Mac's wisdom:

"Ladies, when you date, stop trying to be your man's mama. I see it every day. Don't nobody want to make love to their mama!"

46

LATANYA & SAMUEL L. JACKSON

Accomplished actors LaTanya Richardson Jackson and Samuel L. Jackson began dating in the early 1970's while both were college students in Atlanta. After graduating with degrees in theater, the dynamic couple moved to New York City to pursue acting careers. Married more than 23 years, they have survived stormy times and wounded hearts, but with love and healing, their union is stronger than ever.

Total attraction:

LaTanya—"Sam is the finest MF that ever walked the face of the earth. And he is kind, with a good heart."

Sam—"The first thing I noticed about LaTanya was that she was black. Then came the smile and the energy she projected. And I love her spirit."

Surviving marital setbacks:

Sam—"When I was that crazy addict, it would have been easy for her to have gotten out of the relationship. Then, when I came back from rehab, it was all about me, me, me. And I would get with somebody, and when the sex was over, it was like, 'Now what?' I don't want to have to pay the rest of my life because I was trying to have fun one night. I'm so pleased that my family has been saved."

LaTanya—"I stayed with him because I had to. I made a promise to God that I would be there. I wasn't going to let him die. When it comes to affairs, you end up saying, 'Do they have a stopping point?' I think they did. But he's had to forgive me, too. I've had to learn the importance of guarding my tongue."

Why their union lasts:

LaTanya—"We have great sex and a belief in something greater than ourselves— faith in God. So many times we've had to roll stuff over into the spiritual realm and let it be taken care of there."

Sam—"I have a strong sense of family. It has to do with how I was raised. We have Zoe, and I firmly believe that kids deserve and need two parents."

Their wisdom:

LaTanya—"If you confront problems in the physical world, you might hurt somebody or hurt yourself, so move things over into the spiritual world."

Sam—"I'm grateful my life has been saved, and my family has survived."

LET LOVE RULE

Love nourishes the soul. It heals and fortifies us, and is everywhere around us. All of nature is love. We are meant to experience the joy of love in our intimate relationships, and even in our everyday interaction with people we may never see again. Embrace every opportunity to love that life offers, and you will experience the richness and beauty of living.

8 TIPS FOR KEEPING LOVE ALIVE

A loving relationship sometimes needs a little extra kindling to keep the flame alive:

Keep your partner high on your to-do list. Connect deeply every day for at least a few minutes—smiling, hugging and touching to say I love you. No matter how many children or chores you may have, regularly make time for each other.

Keep clearing the air. Pay attention to what your relationship needs. Even when the time is ripe for romance, unresolved issues and past-due apologies can make igniting passion next to impossible. Check in with each other frequently to clear the air.

Vent gently. Try not to blame or criticize, but to speak openly and honestly about your own feelings. Remember, our relationships are mirrors. They show us where we need to help ourselves.

Address your issues. If wounds have gone unattended for too long and anger has set in, professional help may be needed to forgive and get back on a loving course. Rediscover what first attracted you to your partner.

Keep evolving and growing. Be your own best friend and keep trying new things. Do what delights you—learning languages, playing instruments and sports, whatever brings you joy. Take the pressure of pleasing you off your relationship—a partnership is icing on the cake.

Develop nurturing rituals. Take walks together, trade foot and shoulder massages, make time for "night talk." All these things increase intimacy.

Pray together. Deepen your spiritual union: Establish the practice of talking to the Creator together.

Talk, talk, talk. Touch, touch, touch. More, more, more.

7 STEPS TO A MORE LOVING FAMILY

Truth be told, all families are riddled with drama in varying degrees. But with love, patience and lots of compassion, we can make ours a safe haven that provides all its members with joy and comfort. Follow these steps:

Make communication a family ritual. With our busy lives, we can often forget to listen to those who are closest to us. We may bark orders or express our dislikes with little regard for the feelings of others. Make a conscious effort to listen, even if you don't like what you're hearing. Hold your tongue and try not to criticize.

Stay connected. Plan to share a meal each day with your family, and turn off the radio and television so that you can tune in to one another. When family members are spread out across the country, you can still be close. Organize family get-togethers—time to share and reconnect. And, of course, you can visit frequently on-line.

Expose your children to a breadth of cultures. It's our responsibility as parents to teach our children how to live with confidence and courage in the world. There is so much richness all around us—in our community and beyond. Start where you are and explore your neighborhood with your children. Venture to neighboring communities and see how others live, what they eat, what languages they may speak. Expose your children to fine music from jazz to African drumming, classical to opera.

Lower the volume on your anger. Family gatherings easily call up all our wounds and can descend into full-throttle screaming matches. Don't take to heart anyone's negativity. Make the commitment to not raise your voice, and to discuss rather than argue. Walk away before you say something that you cannot take back. Resist the urge to scream in front of children, and try to shield them from angry exchanges.

Encourage quiet time. Often families are caught up in a whirlwind of activities. Plan downtime together. Teach children the value of silence and reflection. Make a big deal out of the time they spend reading, drawing or doing quiet activities.

Leave no stone unturned. Family dramas do not have to be set in stone. You have the power to change negative dynamics. If actions of a relative trouble you, maybe it's time to call in a mediator such as a wise elder or counselor to help the family through the difficulties. For everyone's sake, do not be ashamed to ask for help.

Live your life fully. Shortchanging yourself doesn't help anyone and it hurts you deeply, weakening your effectiveness and ability to help others. When you put your happiness first, everyone around you benefits.

"When you have success, it's not about ego. You're just saying, 'Thank you, God, for using me.'"

— INDIA.ARIE

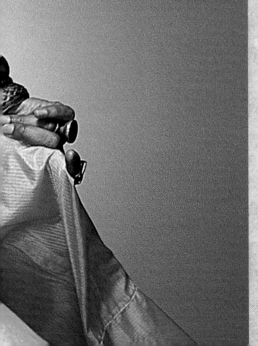

KEEPING THE FAITH

JACQUELINE PETERS CANNON

Ever since the 1960's, Jacqueline Peters Cannon has been a student of metaphysics—
the science of mind–body connection. Although she earned her master's degree in
nursing from Yale, Cannon has her own practice as a holistic counselor and educator,
helping clients solve their physical challenges by getting in touch with their spiritual
and emotional selves. She is a devoted community worker, and in 2002, she became a
part-time model.

Mind and body:

"My ideas on spirituality and health have been the same for the past 30 years.
Healing is spiritual. I handle any physical or emotional challenges through prayer.
It works and it heals."

Personal growth:

"As a young wife and mother, my concerns were mostly material. But as I matured
and developed my spiritual life, my whole sense of materiality has changed,
and is still changing."

Self-preservation strategy:

"They say you are what you eat, but I say you are what you think. I believe we all
have the ability to empower ourselves by our thoughts. I base everything I do on
that principle."

Stress busters:

"The moment I feel stressed, I know I have gone off on a tangent, and I pull myself
back with deep breathing, reading and listening to music."

What matters:

"The most important thing in my life is being a mother and a grandmother. My
son died at 33 eight years ago, and my faith is what has carried me through."

Cannon's wisdom:

"If you develop a spiritual path, everything else will fall into place."

34

75

48

DENZEL WASHINGTON

In two decades, Academy Award–winning actor and director Denzel Washington has become a big-screen icon. He never seems shaken, never gives less than his best work and never stops moving forward. The son of a minister, he has a life that's a successful blend of work, family and faith.

The blessings of family:

"At the end of the day, acting is making a living, but it *ain't*. My biggest triumphs were when each of my four children was born. Pauletta and I have a real partnership, but what I'm impressed with the most is the way she has raised our children. My son went off to college with a Bible in his suitcase."

Fathers are crucial:

"I would say to Black women who are raising sons alone: 'Don't cut them off from their fathers, whatever the issues are between you.' Sons need fathers, and they're going to find them in one way or another. A lot of the problems young men have out in the streets are really about boys trying to find their fathers and coming to some understanding of manhood. Without a good father, they'll look for that understanding in the worst places."

Helping children develop:

"I love watching children grow and develop. Before I started acting, I worked with the Boys' Club and the YMCA. I coached my children and other people's children. Now, in a sense, I apply that passion to filmmaking."

Focusing on the positive:

"We're in a time of spiritual warfare. A lot of people have done wrong for a long time. Maybe that's why I made the *Antwone Fisher* film —to try to stand against the turmoil in the world. In whatever small way, we've got to share some of the good stories so we can say, 'Hey, you can have problems, you can struggle, but you can still survive. You can still win.' "

Choosing goodness:

"The bottom line is that I'm trying to do good. I want to stand for good. I'm not saying I'm anybody's saint, now. I'm sure not. But I am trying."

Washington's wisdom:

"We've all been given a gift. The challenge is to figure out what you're going to do with what you've been given and to stand for good."

INDIA.ARIE

As one of only a few Black children in a small town in Colorado, singer India.Arie felt out of place. And after her parents divorced and she moved to Atlanta with her mother, she felt like an outsider among Black kids. It wasn't until she went away to study jewelry making at Savannah College of Art and Design that she began to evolve into the young woman who now can lift her voice about loving every part of herself.

The heartbreak of skin problems:

"At age 13, because of severe acne, makeup was my medicine. I would wear it just to look normal. I may have wanted to go to a football game, but I was afraid that my makeup made me look like I was wearing a mask, so I just wouldn't go."

Loving herself:

"Around the time I turned 20, I made a conscious decision to change, and I became a vegan—eating no animal products—to remedy the difficulties with my complexion. That was a pivotal point for me."

Her own rules:

"I'm going to do whatever I want to do. I'm not going to wear makeup or do anything to my hair if I don't want to. I'm just going to accept the fact that this is how I look, love it and do what's best for me."

You can't hurry love:

"I'm waiting for someone I can give my love to and not be afraid that he won't give it back. I don't just want a boyfriend—I could have five boyfriends. I want someone who is part of my destiny."

Message in the music:

"I'm on my spiritual path, and my songs are messages to myself. I want people to know that I'm still growing. I want angels to speak through me and my music so that I can bring wisdom to people. When you think of it that way, even when you do have success, it's not about ego gratification. You're just saying, 'Thank you, God, for using me.'"

India.Arie's wisdom:

"Don't conform to how others want you to act and how they want you to look. Stand firmly in your own power and beauty."

27

KEEPING THE FAITH

58

SANDRA REED

Sandra Reed is a woman with a plan. The Oakland-based grandmother is not only a software consultant but has also begun exploring motivational speaking and commercial acting. And a constant priority in her life is her commitment to her physical and spiritual well-being.

Staying centered:

"The first thing in the morning, I devote time to reading spiritual books. Then sometimes I write in my journal, or I sit and reflect on a passage. I do yoga and meditate. I leave for the day feeling filled with joy and excited about life."

Traveling companions:

"God and water are my constant companions. In college I had hepatitis. The doctor told me to drink water, and long before it was fashionable, I started a lifelong habit of drinking about a gallon a day. I keep bottles of water in my car, and I always keep a spiritual book in my handbag, so if I'm stuck in traffic or on a long trip, instead of cursing, I am getting positive reinforcement and going with the flow."

Relationship priorities:

"I try to give unconditional love to everyone. I am open to dating, but I am so comfortable with myself that a relationship is not a priority. I am not looking outside of myself for another individual to give me love or joy. I have learned to be my own best friend. My priority is to stay in touch with my inner self, and I work on growing better every day."

Finding yourself:

"I have learned to not give my power away. Once you know that you are love, peace and joy—and you can't fail—that is who you will be."

Reed's wisdom:

"Stay away from toxic people and toxic situations. Love them—but from afar."

YRESE

We've watched Tyrese Gibson mature from a young man in a popular cola commercial to the platinum-selling singer and actor he is today. Yet what most of us don't know about the former Watts, Los Angeles, native is that he takes pride in his spiritual development and in his Tyrese Gibson Watts Foundation.

Finding his faith:

"I was never happy about any of the churches I attended until I found AME in Los Angeles. I realized that the minister was a man connected to God, and I found a place where I could clearly hear the message."

Finding a mentor:

"When I met John Bryant, founder of Operation Hope, a Los Angeles economic-development organization, I had many unanswered questions about starting my own organization to help the youth in Watts. Although John had a full schedule and enormous commitments, and he was exhausted, he gave me his time so generously. I am in awe of this man who has more knowledge than anyone I've ever met. John is my mentor, and I love him dearly. I have called on him during my weakest moments."

Focused mission:

"I'm not a perfect man, but I have accomplished a lot. I have been blessed, and I'm very aware of the responsibility that comes with that. Now I focus on passing on whatever I can to young Black people in my community. John told me that I am a child of God, and God is using me to bring hope to those who are uninspired or who feel there is nothing left to aspire to. Knowing that my organization has made a difference in Watts helps me sleep better at night."

Taking on greatness:

"I believe that you can never take a break from greatness—and relationships offer the highest opportunity for achieving greatness. As soon as you take them for granted, you have problems. I'm vigilant about showing great appreciation to the people in my life."

Gibson's wisdom:

"We all have a chance to create a better life. Be aware of what you need to do to get ahead, and get out of your own way."

25

KEEPING THE FAITH

T.D. Jakes

Television evangelist, best-selling author and pastor to a flock of millions, Bishop T.D. Jakes delivers messages that are therapy for the spirit. The charismatic founder of Potter's House, the megachurch in Dallas, inspires, teaches and counsels that God heals all wounds. A native of West Virginia, Bishop Jakes believes we can put our families on firm ground, no matter what our challenges.

Prescription for the Black family:

"Our traditional family values—standing by our families, taking care of the elderly, helping our children, especially in times of crisis—have been challenged by the pressures of contemporary society. When you get caught up in the fast pace of life, it's easy to lose purpose, and this has eroded the Black family to its core. In addition, slavery was a trauma that systematically destroyed the family unit. Modern African-Americans don't want to hear this; they'd rather move beyond the subject. But we can't move beyond it until we understand it."

Redefining family:

"Our family may not be ideal; we all have flaws. But if the commitment among family members is strong enough, it can accommodate their dysfunctions. We all need somebody who won't run from our afflictions—that's the role family plays. We have to keep remembering, it's my son, my daughter, my husband, my wife. Regardless of the problem, we all need a safe place to get well."

Can't buy happiness:

"Financial success and happiness aren't necessarily part of the same package. It's possible for you to be at the height of your career and be as miserable as you have ever been. In fact, I think many of us were happier when we were spitting watermelon seeds off Grandma's back porch. At least then we had the acceptance and the support system of family."

Women's dilemmas:

"Women seem to be asking themselves, *How do I relate to my companion, my children and my career, and still have a healthy relationship with my faith and myself?* How does a woman respond appropriately to the many expectations people have of her without becoming spiritually bankrupt?"

Jakes's wisdom:

"Believe in God. Build yourself up. Have standards that you won't go below. That way you can come into all your relationships from a position of strength."

47

OPHELIA BAKON

When Ophelia Bakon was in her mid-twenties, she faced the challenges of an abusive marriage, a divorce and the prospect of raising three sons. She also suffered an obstruction, which landed her in the hospital. There she had time to be still—and think about the direction she'd like her life to take. Now, three decades later, she co-owns a boutique with three of her sisters and helps run concert-promotion and event-planning businesses. Her sister, Evelyn, appears on page 126.

Precious intuition:

"I was in the hospital for three and a half weeks. I was sure I was going to die. So I started praying, and received great comfort from that. Then my mother brought me a copy of the *Daily Word*, and reading it taught me about the power of the mind and made me stronger and fearless! There's something inside each one of us that's so wonderful if you know how to listen to it."

Sisterly love:

"My four sisters and I are all best friends, and we have a lot of faith. We work together and travel together. If there's something we want to do, we take that deep breath, and we do it."

Mother knows best:

"Viola Bakon raised us for the real world. I was always looking elsewhere for something. Mom said, 'Girl, stop looking over there. What you're looking for is right inside you.'"

Bakon's wisdom:

"Be open to wherever spirit leads you. When your heart is open, it's open to the whole world and you just soar!"

56

54

GAIL FELTON

Gail Felton can point with pride to a life of accomplishments. The Philadelphia native is a financial planner and grandmother of two, and in 2000 she was Ms. Delaware County in the Ms. USA pageant. Felton has also faced three of life's toughest challenges: illness, the death of a parent and divorce. But with strength, courage and a positive attitude, she has withstood the tests.

Her illness:

"A few years ago I was sick and in the hospital for two months. Due to an obstruction, a foot of my intestine had to be removed. It was pretty bad. I was in intensive care for a week, on a feeding tube, and I went from 118 to 99 pounds. But here I am today, standing strong."

A secret revealed:

"The cancer my mom had been fighting for eight years worsened during my long hospital stay. Knowing she needed me spurred my recovery. Mom always gave me strength. Shortly after getting out of the hospital, I was taking care of Mom. She told me one night she had seen white spiders. I saw them as a sign from God and said, 'Mom, they're angels.' She passed away soon after."

Attitude of gratitude:

"Even when Mom was sick and in a lot of pain, she still would say you have to be thankful for every day. I may not go to church every Sunday, but every day of my life I thank God."

Stress strategy:

"I had a really tough two years, and now I have decided not to put stress on myself. I don't worry about things I can't control."

In solitude:

"I take mineral baths for an hour at a time. I use the private time to think about life, where I'm going and what I want to do next."

Felton's wisdom:

"Love yourself, and you'll feel better. Don't worry about the small things."

TRUST IN THE DIVINE PLAN

Our lives need constant nourishment and "weeding" to flourish. And despite the challenges and changes we will face over the years, each of us can remain resilient and strong. Through faith and prayer and practicing the time-honored principles of love and forgiveness, each of us can tap into the power God has bequeathed us—and thrive.

5 STEPS TO PEACE AND HARMONY

We can enjoy a sense of grounding, even when the world around us is spinning out of control. Here's how:

Pray and have faith. Spirituality is about the inner work. Seek a deep personal relationship with God. We simply need to be still and listen, and heed the wisdom of the Holy Spirit, which will always put us on the divine-right track.

Surround yourself with positive people. Phase out those who always seem to come with a side order of drama and negativity. The people in your life should show by their actions that they like you. They should be supportive of your aspirations and be moving in the same direction as you.

Give to others. Make time to volunteer or enrich someone else's life. There is no better way to nourish your spirit than to lift the spirit of another. Whether you tithe, listen with an understanding ear or give to someone in need, be sure to give willingly and wholeheartedly.

Forgive. Holding on to old resentment blocks the love and light from flowing your way. Take the high road: That's where the joy in life is. Be compassionate, and pray for those who have done you wrong. Remember how important it was for you to feel forgiven for your own mistakes. So commit to giving those who have hurt you the same grace and mercy you need.

Give love. Let God's love shine through you to all you meet and interact with. Practice loving others through mishaps and their faults and shortcomings. Essential to this is practicing loving and accepting all that you are—your body, mind and soul, hair, skin, unique features and color. This is the most healing and most important work we must do all of our lives.

WHERE TWO OR MORE ARE GATHERED...

Consider organizing a prayer group or healing circle. This is a powerful way to help others—the sick-and-shut-in sister around the corner, the family whose mother just passed away, a community devastated by a hurricane. Here are some tips on setting up a group.

Attract like-minded people. Decide how large or small a group you want and go about finding the people. Spread the word through a circle of friends or place notices in a house of worship or community bulletins—state what you want to do and the kind of members you're looking for. Believe that when you do good deeds, the divine-right people show up to help in the effort.

Make everyone feel welcome. Share and take turns talking about your beliefs in spirituality and God. Get to know one another.

Decide on your mission. Will you pray for individuals everyone knows and for

your community? Or will you pray for large groups of people you may never meet, such as suffering children throughout the world? Will the group also help beyond prayer—supporting people on a more personal level, like making hospital visits? And, if so, will you visit people as a group or individually? Will you make calls or send letters and cards? Decide on ways in which you want prayer to heal the lives of others.

Ask for help. Starting a group doesn't mean you must become its leader. There are a myriad of ways to organize. You may decide to rotate leading the group among all members, invite a divinity student to a play a chief role, or on occasion ask local spiritual leaders who are experts in grief counseling or working with the elderly, HIV/AIDS patients or troubled teens to join you.

"The more I work out, the more I enjoy it."

— MORJORIE NEWLIN

SHAPING UP

LETTICE GRAHAM

At age 79 Lettice Graham was crowned queen of New York's Golden Image senior beauty pageant. Two years later, as captain of the Harlem Honeys and Bears swim team, she competed in water-ballet events throughout the city. For Graham, a widow and retired AT&T representative, her healthy lifestyle remains front and center.

Her workout routine:

"I learned to swim at 64, and I go to the pool for two and a half hours, five days a week. Swimming keeps my body toned. I also do yoga every morning to strengthen my bones and keep flexible. And I go line dancing every Friday night."

What she eats:

"I grew up on a farm in Jacksonville, North Carolina, so I am a stickler for fresh food. After my swim, I go to the senior citizen center and have a nice healthy lunch, mostly chicken or fish. My dinners are usually light, simple and nutritious. I might put a bunch of fresh celery in a pot with chicken broth, turkey pastrami and rice to stew for a while. I don't fry foods."

On staying healthy:

"I have an orange every day, for the vitamin C. I can't remember the last time I had a cold. I also eat an apple. Then I take my multivitamin and vitamin E and a cod-liver oil capsule, which keeps my joints loose."

General philosophy:

"Happiness is a state of mind. It's about how you feel about yourself. My parents always made sure I had what I needed. I never confused my wants with my needs, and, believe me, I feel very blessed. At 81, I take no medication and I have no pain."

Graham's wisdom:

"Don't deny yourself what you like to eat, but eat in moderation. Use your scale—but don't be discouraged by the number."

81

SHEMAR MOORE

After being spotted in GQ *magazine in 1993 by a casting agent, Shemar Moore landed his first acting role—on the television soap opera* The Young and the Restless. *That seven-year run led to hosting* Soul Train *and then to feature-film roles. The former athlete stays fit, firm and passionate about his exercise regimen.*

Swinging for success:

"My uncle Steven Wilson, who played semipro baseball in Boston, put me in my first Junior League team. Although I was terrible at first, I eventually got a baseball scholarship at Santa Clara University, where I had baseball practice five days a week, four hours a day. To this day, I work out for at least two hours, five days a week."

Hollywood-style shape-up:

"The camera makes you look much heavier, so you don't want your body to distract people from the role you are playing. When I exercise, I feel better and think more clearly. I know my body, and there is a certain rhythm to my workouts—45 minutes of cardio; 90 minutes of weight lifting for biceps, triceps, thighs and buttocks; 600 sit-ups and lots of stretching. I lift light weights with high repetitions to stay lean and cut."

On a mission:

"I exercise by myself because it's work—not a social experience. My friends call me a beast in the gym. I am hard on myself and always pushing the limit. I box with a trainer and like high-impact hiking, doing three to five miles running up hills."

The comfort zone:

"As a kid, I went through stages of being chubby. I love to eat it all—like chicken and waffles—so I have to make an effort to keep my weight down. When I'm not working, I gain about ten pounds. But I stay away from sodas and sugar. Excessive carbohydrates cause my body to hold on to extra weight. When I get into work mode, I cut those things out."

Moore's wisdom:

"Not everything is about Hollywood or looking good. It's about travel, knowledge and fueling yourself to become a better person."

33

HILDA STEPHENSON

Hilda Stephenson has had her share of health challenges. She suffers from hypertension and has had a bout with a painful disease. Yet that hasn't prevented her from being active, staying fit and keeping the faith. Stephenson and her daughter, 68-year-old Beverly Taylor, who appears on page 136, are ageless beauties who live healthful lifestyles. Today Stephenson still rises at 5:00 every morning to fit exercise into her busy days.

Exercise ethics:

"Ever since I was a little girl, exercising has been important to me. And I was born in 1913, way before people figured out that exercising is important. Early on, I started doing splits—something you never saw polite Black girls doing. I was around 9 when my brother told me that if I stood on my head, I would never have to worry about my hair falling out, so I started standing on my head, and I loved it! It was years before I figured out that he didn't know what he was talking about, but I kept doing it anyway—until I was 86."

Eating for eternal health:

"When I lived in New York, I would never eat with my coworkers. I would spend my lunch hour walking while I munched on carrot and celery sticks. They would sit up there eating fried chicken and call me the lady with the grass. All the fruits and vegetables I eat aid my digestion. I never have any problems."

Senior moves:

"For the past 30 years I have exercised alone in the morning. Today I also derive enjoyment from exercising with others. Now I make sure to get out of my house at 8:00 so I can get to my 9:30 aerobics class. Twice a week I go to water-aerobics classes, and then I go walking."

Stephenson's wisdom:

"There is nothing in the world like having girlfriends. They keep you young."

90

ERNESTINE SHEPHERD

After 31 years in corporate America as an education professional, Ernestine Shepherd retired and began working part-time as a teacher. Today she's also a weight-training instructor and enters bodybuilding competitions. For her sixty-seventh birthday she gave herself the ultimate fitness gift: She trimmed her already low percentage of body fat from 19 to 15 percent by training for the Baltimore Marathon—a 26.2-mile race that she had already won in her age category in 2001.

Finding fitness:

"When I was 56, my sister, Blackwell, who is a year older, and I went to buy bathing suits for a church picnic. We tried on various suits and burst out laughing when we looked at ourselves in the full-length mirror. We knew it was high time to take better care of our bodies and hightailed it to a fitness center, where we began doing aerobics."

Getting in serious shape:

"We were the oldest clients at the gym, but after we'd done one year of aerobics, the trainer took notice of how much progress we were making and suggested that we begin lifting weights. In no time, we were developing our muscles."

Struck by tragedy:

"One day while we were weight-training I noticed that my sister had cotton in her ears. She said she had gotten water in her ears while swimming. Blackwell had never been sick a day in her life, but a week later she was in a coma. She died from a brain aneurysm and I was completely devastated."

Surviving the setback:

"Six months after I lost Blackwell, my dear friend, Raymond, encouraged me to take care of myself and get back to the gym. Now, I get up at 4:00 every morning to racewalk outdoors until 6:00, and I do weight training in the evenings."

Shepherd's wisdom:

"You only live once. Get up and go after what you want."

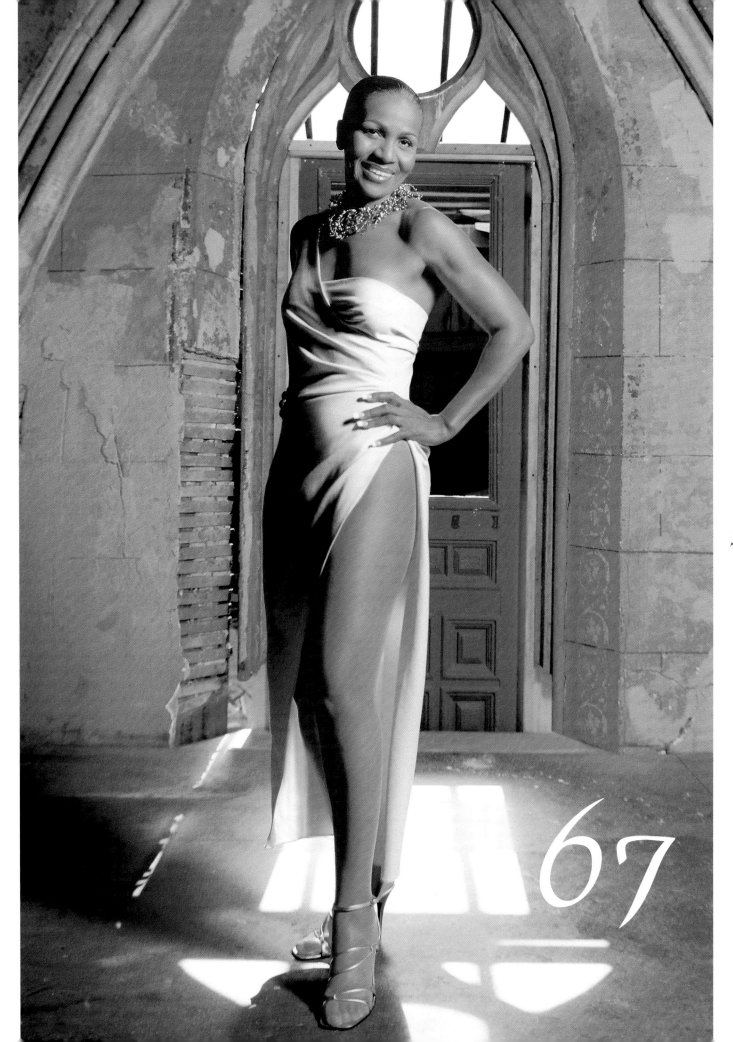

67

83

MORJORIE NEWLIN

Retired nurse Morjorie Newlin is living proof that age ain't nothing but a number. In 1993, when she turned 72, she began working out to offset osteoporosis, the weakening of bones. Bit by the fitness bug, Newlin started participating in body-building competitions around the country, and now she has more than 25 trophies perched on her mantel.

All the right moves:

"I work out four days a week. I usually warm up on the treadmill for 45 minutes, then do aerobics for cardiovascular fitness. Next I lift weights, working on different parts of my body on alternate days."

Feeling fit:

"I started lifting weights so I could be stronger. I didn't want my children to have to take care of me. And the more I worked out, the more I enjoyed it. Then my trainer talked me into competing. I like doing my routine to 'Respect' by Aretha Franklin. I really feel that song when I'm out there onstage. The crowd goes wild! I'm not concerned with winning first prize. It's just important to be able to master a skill."

Age-defying advice:

"It's not a bad thing to be concerned with how you look. And it's not about being pretty, but about keeping up your appearance. It's important to do cardiovascular exercise for heart health, weight training to keep bones and muscles strong, and stretching to stay limber. I feel good every day that I am not a burden to my family."

Celebrating family:

"One weekend recently my great-grandchildren were celebrating birthdays, and my daughter planned a big day for them. There were 15 of us, and I looked around and saw the four generations of family together—and I felt blessed to be alive and well, and excited about fully living every single day."

Newlin's wisdom:

"It's essential to do as much as you possibly can to remain healthy and strong so that you can maintain your independence."

$\mathcal{A}$ISHA JACKSON

When it comes to maintaining the well-being of herself and others, physical therapist and lecturer Aisha Jackson doesn't rest on her laurels. In 2003 the Washington, D.C., native competed in the National Aerobics Championship Fitness Challenge. She's also actively spreading her health message.

Shifting career gears:

"I am so proud that I went back to school in 1995 to receive my bachelor's degree in physical therapy from Howard University. At the time I was a receptionist and a single mother, so it took an enormous amount of juggling to work, go to school, study, tend to my daughter and maintain my fitness regime—and my sanity!"

Eating for life:

"In 1980 I started to change my diet. I haven't eaten pork or beef in 20 years. Instead, I eat fish, chicken, whole grains, tofu and vegetables."

Strategy for aging:

"Once I reached 50, I received my fitness certification. Now I teach three one-hour cardio-sculpt classes a week in addition to doing my private workouts. My classes begin with intense cardio and end with weight training. Today I am in much better shape than I've ever been."

Food for the soul:

"I get up at 5:00 every morning, and I try to start my day with something that feeds my spiritual self. I read passages from the Bible or from Egyptian philosophy."

Educating our community:

"Diabetes runs in my family and caused my grandmother's death. As a physical therapist I also encounter many patients who have developed complications as a result of diabetes. I'm very concerned about its impact on the African-American community, and that's why I'm intent on educating us about the obesity–diabetes connection and how a fitness regimen can prevent both."

Just for fun:

"My favorite pastime is going to the beach. Sometimes my mother, who is 73, goes with me. When I go to a pool, I swim laps, but for me, being near the ocean and hearing the sound of waves is the most relaxing."

Jackson's wisdom:

"Physical, emotional and spiritual wellness is very important in our lives. We really can't have one without the others."

51

GET UP, GET MOVING, GET IN SHAPE

Imagine your body strong, lean and lively. Hold on to that vision, and accept the fact that with the right fitness moves, you can achieve it. We're not talking about climbing Mount Everest—just the tailor-made moves that will make you, your loved ones and your doctor very happy. Having a fabulous physique is not the only reason to keep fit: It's a proven medical fact that a workout a day keeps illness away. Diabetes, cardiovascular disease and hypertension are just a few of the ailments that can come from not exercising—conditions that have devastated our families and communities. So get up and get fit—starting today.

PUT FITNESS FIRST

You don't have to run. You can dance, swim, do tai chi, ride a bike or walk. Just get moving at least three times a week for 30 minutes or more, and don't forget to warm up to help prevent injuries and to stretch after exercising to keep you supple. Resistance training improves your strength and immune system, and it staves off osteoporosis. So work out with weights.

POWER WALKING
With upper torso slightly forward, abs contracted, pump arms and step with a strong heel-toe action for 30 minutes, outdoors or on a treadmill.

Cardiovascular

A

B

EXPLOSIVE MOVE

Begin with knees bent, arms crossed as shown left (A). Then burst open, up on your toes, in jumping-jack fashion as shown below (B). Do 3 sets of 5 to 12 repetitions.

JUMPING ROPE

Turn the rope using your wrists and forearms only, and jump for as long as you can—five minutes or more. Remember to stay up on your toes.

Strength

PUSH-UP

With hands shoulder width apart, exhale and inhale; bend arms to lower body. Do 3 sets of 5 to 12 reps.

CRUNCH

With lower back pressed down, knees bent and fingers behind ears, breathe in, then exhale as you lift shoulders off the floor. Do 3 sets of 8 to 12 crunches.

LEG LIFT

With one hand on a chair, inhale. Exhale as you flex foot, lift leg and bend knee up and down (A). Then lift leg sideways and back (B). Do 3 sets of 8 to 12 reps; switch sides.

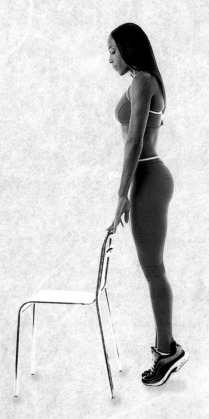

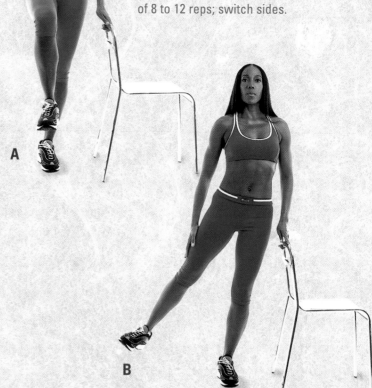

A

B

CALF RAISE

Holding on to a chair for support, roll up on your toes. Hold, then bring heels down. Do 3 sets of 12 to 24 reps.

BICEPS CURL

With feet together, knees slightly bent, hold a light weight, palm toward body. Rotate palm up as you lift. Alternate arms for 8 to 12 reps, 3 sets.

TRICEPS KICKBACK

Feet together, knees bent, lean forward as shown. Begin with left arm bent 90 degrees; then straighten. Do 3 sets of 8 to 12 reps.

Cool Down

STRETCHING

Sit up with legs bent as shown. Inhale and, leading with left arm, stretch to the right, resting on right arm. Hold; repeat 4 to 8 times. Switch sides.

SHAPING UP

"There are going to
be disappointments,
but we can rise
above them."

— HOPE FISHER

OVERCOMING

HALLE BERRY

One of the most sought-after film actresses in Hollywood, Halle Berry reached a career pinnacle when she became the first Black woman to win an Academy Award for Best Actress in 2002. But she has had to climb other mountains as well—living with diabetes, violence in her childhood, challenges in her love life. Through it all, she has learned that healing is always possible.

Seeking help when you hurt:

"When I was 10, I was enraged, frightened and confused by the disastrous return of my father, a violent man. My wonderful mother saw that my mental state—as well as my sister's—was at risk, and she quickly placed us in psychotherapy to make sure we had an appropriate outlet for discussing our feelings. What a gift!"

Looking inward:

"I was lucky to learn at such an early age that there is a calm, effective way to process emotions, and it is a lesson I've never forgotten. I've continued in therapy, and that keeps me grounded. I still ask myself tough questions: *How do I turn from rage to reason? What am I supposed to learn here? How will this crisis contribute to my growth?*"

Coping with heartbreak:

"All romantic relationships suffer crises. No woman alive can claim otherwise. And all our crises are heartbreaking. They may be different, but the common thread is far more significant. And the challenge is how we react: What do we do? Where do we take our feelings? How do we process the pain?"

It takes two to heal:

"In a relationship I can work on myself all day long, but if my partner refuses to do his work—to look at his own complex patterns of behavior—growth as a couple is impossible."

Berry's wisdom:

"To process your feelings and examine your issues, seek professional help when you're hurting—and to hell with anyone's objection!"

35

OVERCOMING

MADELEINE MOORE

After the 911 tragedy, advertising and marketing entrepreneur Madeleine Moore changed the direction of her company toward building a legacy in our communities. She convinced her major clients to underwrite cause-related initiatives—such as testing for prostate cancer and glaucoma. It is her goal to help others overcome challenges, as she has done in her own life.

Childhood challenge:

"My mother died of kidney disease at the age of 36. I was 18 years old and had to quickly become the caretaker of my 6-month-old brother and 18-month-old sister. I watched as my bereft father turned to alcohol, so I put my college plans on hold in order to develop the muscles to jump in and do some heavy lifting for my family."

Support network:

"My high school girlfriends rallied around me and taught me everything—from changing diapers to cleaning and cooking. It was through their love and support that I learned how to run a household."

New beginning:

"Going through a divorce in 1985 after ten years of marriage was tremendously difficult. I went through a healing process in a program that taught me about the power of free will and choice. I transformed myself from a mousy wife into a bodacious entrepreneur, started my own firm and faced the fear of raising my son on my own. I learned that I was much stronger emotionally than I thought I was."

Moore's wisdom:

"You can create the life you want. Set your sights on your goal and believe you can achieve it."

63

CURTIS MARTIN

Seeing Curtis Martin today, it appears that life has always been good for the premier running back of the New York Jets. His career is in high gear. But life hasn't always been this good for Martin. It has taken years of self-reflection, faith and building of inner strength to get him to this point. Martin's life has been one of death, despair, anger, awakening and triumph.

A tragic past:

"When I was 9 years old, my mother and I found my grandmother dead in her bed with a butcher knife embedded in her chest. Four years later, my aunt Carol was killed, and when my mother got home from work, I had to break the terrible news to her. I have known at least 30 friends, family members or associates who have been killed."

Building a cold heart:

"With a father who was in and out of the crazy house and strung out on drugs, combined with a mother who was being physically, mentally and emotionally tortured by him—and oftentimes taking it out on me—I had the ingredients for a coldhearted, gotta-do-what-I-gotta-do-to-survive, daredevil teenager. I felt, *Life isn't fair anyway, so f--- it.*"

The defining moment:

"By age 20, I was burned out. I was tormented by the nightmare that someone was trying to kill me. I barely slept. One day I went to the nearest church, sat down and said, 'God, I don't know anything about you or this Jesus cat, but if you just let me breathe, I'll do whatever you want me to do.'"

A bright future:

"The birth of my godchild, Diamond, was the extra push I needed to get my life in order. God cracked that shell off my heart and took away my hardness and defense mechanisms. Thanks to a change in my thoughts, my heart and ultimately how I was living my life, I now have peace, and I love living. I'm more responsible in my thoughts, my motives, my words and my actions. Because change is a process and not simply an event, I'm grateful to God for being patient with me."

Martin's wisdom:

"Our lives are the sum total of the decisions we have or have not made."

30

61

CHARSIE J. HERNDON

Charsie J. Herndon has worn many hats in her lifetime. She has been a lawyer, a motivational speaker and a bodybuilding champion. Now the director of government employee fitness in Fulton County, Georgia, Herndon has relied on her spiritual grounding to overcome the loss of her mother and to discover a new life and love.

Losing a loved one:

"I am an only child, and my mother and I had always been tight. She was my buddy, my girlfriend, my confidante. Before she passed away I had been commuting by car from Atlanta to Durham, North Carolina, to relieve her caregivers and to make sure she was properly cared for. I wasn't aware of the toll her illness and death had taken on me until months after she passed away. I internalized the loss and began to lose my appetite."

Healing the pain:

"It was a challenge. I had to dig deep to find a way to regain my health and strength. One day I asked God to show me a way to restore myself, and I just started eating again. I've gained my weight back and I am pumping iron. One thing that is universal is the presence and the power of the Almighty God. When trauma enters your life, you have a tendency to forget that, but the source is there, and it never leaves."

Late-life romance:

"If someone told me that romance could look and feel this good at 60, I would call them a liar. With wisdom there is no reason to put up with a lot of jigginess, to use a youthful term. You learn to take the bitter with the sweet. You learn to embrace the happy moments and grow and live with them."

Self-preservation strategy:

"I have quiet time, moments when I meditate and count my blessings."

Herndon's wisdom:

"Everyone has her own journey, and there is no one answer or one way to do it."

ONICA

Monica Arnold's illustrious recording career has garnered her sales of more than 10 million albums and a Grammy award. But over the past few years, on the personal side, her resilience has been truly tested. Within a few months, her beloved grandmother passed; her closest friend, Selena, died from an aneurysm; and her boyfriend, Jarvis, committed suicide. After three years of healing, Monica has emerged stronger, sharing her pain and joy through her music.

Losing her lover:

"In July 2000 my boyfriend decided he didn't want to live anymore. He was distraught about his brother's death, and he had lost faith in his professional dreams. He saw no other way out. I wasn't part of the problem, and unfortunately, I couldn't be part of the solution."

The lessons learned:

"Losing Jarvis changed my life. I started to see through all the phony people who were using me. I cut them all off, and that allowed me to focus on those who genuinely love me. When it was all about lights, camera, action, there were people who were always calling. But when trouble arrived, these people couldn't be found. So I cleared the slate."

New life strategies:

"I realize that I cannot control life, and I'm prepared for whatever changes occur. Most people have a ten-year plan. I have learned that life doesn't work that way. I no longer put a time frame on my goals."

Her saving grace:

"I have a strong family. Their spiritual guidance comforted me in my time of need. My stepfather is a Methodist minister. I can always pick up the phone and ask him to pray for me. If you have people who firmly believe in you, they don't have to be right in front of you to serve as inspiration—their prayers will reach you."

Dealing with pain:

"God doesn't put any more on me than I can handle. As a teenager, I strayed from my religious upbringing, but my tragic experiences have put me back in check. I didn't hide from my feelings. I cried, dealt with them and healed. Now I have a stronger message to share."

Monica's wisdom:

"So many people tell us what we can and cannot do. It requires complete focus. We can overcome—our dreams will be realized."

22

Hope Fisher

Before retirement, Hope Fisher was a secretary in the fashion industry. These days her stimulation comes from being active in her community. And this great-grandmother loves to walk, listen to jazz and dance.

Early years:

"When I was growing up, I was very sickly, so I had to keep my resistance up by exercising, getting my rest and watching what I ate. Having health problems during childhood set the tone for how I would take care of myself for the rest of my life."

In her corner:

"My mother really helped me keep a positive outlook. I don't think I would have lived to this age if my mother had not been so supportive of me when I was sick as a child. And I believe in God. When I was 6 years old, three men came to the side of my bed. They knelt by my bed and said they were there to watch over me. I believe I have guardian angels."

Breaking away:

"My first marriage was not very happy, and I knew I could not go on like that. When things are not going right in your marriage, don't sacrifice yourself for the children. If you are not happy, your children feel it, and it affects them. I went to secretarial school because I needed skills so I could leave and become self-supporting."

Fisher's wisdom:

"You have to have a good feeling about life. Then you will grow old gracefully. There are going to be disappointments, but you can rise above them."

77

CARYL MCCALLA

One of the high points of Caryl McCalla's adulthood was sharing communion with the Pope at St. Peter's Basilica in Rome. And each morning on her way to work she stops in at St. Patrick's Cathedral in New York for a moment of reflection and prayer. She works in sales and is a grandmother of three, and despite having a daunting personal experience, she has found peace and is loving life.

Mr. Right?:

"After 20 years of living on my own and raising two children, I met a man — a police officer — who seemed great. Within two months I moved into his house, and we planned to be married. I should have known better than to give up all my stuff — my furniture, my apartment — but I did."

Life's challenge:

"I loaned my boyfriend $42,000 out of my 401(k) to repair his house. He agreed to repay me when he refinanced his home, but instead he gave me an eviction notice. Soon I learned that he had a history of treating women like dirt. He turned out to be a total horror."

Walking by faith:

"I had nowhere to go and no money because $1,000 was deducted from my salary every month to pay back what I had borrowed. I said, 'God has five days to work a miracle,' and I never lost faith. Days before I was to be evicted, a friend offered me an apartment I could afford that had just become vacant at her mother's house. God is wonderful!"

Lessons learned:

"I've learned to follow my first impressions. When I first met this guy, I said, 'He's a jerk.' But he started charming me, and I pushed that thought to the back of my mind. God has told me, 'When I tell you something, listen.'"

Reflections:

"It's been a humbling experience. I had a Jaguar and a fabulous apartment, and now I'm riding buses and trains. It will be a while before I put everything back together, but I have my health, my strength and a job. I'm fortunate that I came out of it with my sanity, and I'm still smiling."

McCalla's wisdom:

"You can't have a testimony without a test. But if you have undying faith, you can come through anything."

58

CAROLE CARTER

When Carole Carter was divorced in 1986, she was 41 years old and had been married for 18 years. At the time her youngest son was 15, and she was a housewife who hadn't worked for five years. Carter summoned all her emotional resources to return to the workplace. She carved out a successful career as a human resources manager, purchased a house, found new love and acquired an enduring passion for fitness.

Surviving divorce:

"It was a devastating blow. My husband had been in charge of everything, and suddenly I had to relearn how to take care of myself and be a strong mother to my two boys. It was an extremely difficult passage in my life. To get through it, I sought the help of a therapist who provided me with coping tools. I was also blessed to be able to rely on good friends. And I was losing weight, looking bad. But that experience was for my highest good. The Lord has guided me to greater blessings."

Road to recovery:

"One day I just decided to let go of the anger, to be prayerful and at peace. Everything fell into place after that."

Finding fitness:

"Ten years ago fitness took center stage in my life. I bought a treadmill, and to this day I exercise on it for 30 minutes, four times a week. I also walk around a beautiful lake and enjoy nature."

A sweet surprise:

"When I moved to Gaithersburg, Maryland, in 1973, I saw a little girl who looked just like my childhood best friend, with whom I had lost touch. It turned out that my friend was her mother. For the last 30 years we have stayed close to each other. Our unconditional sharing makes our bond strong. Having a friend like her and my other longtime girlfriends has meant a lot in my life."

Carter's wisdom:

"You can relate to people on a deeper level when you're spiritually connected. You'll become independent, your own person. You learn the importance of taking care of yourself. In the last ten years I've turned to prayer, and my every need has been met."

57

THROUGH THE FIRE

No matter how great your blessings, beauty, intelligence and talents, you will face adversities that test your very foundation. But remember, pain is the touchstone of spiritual and emotional growth—the mettle that builds character, depth and extraordinary resourcefulness. When we try to sidestep our pain, we become prey to insecurities and addictions, and other self-destructive behaviors that eat away at our psyche and souls. Acknowledge pain and work to heal yourself; you will be rewarded with wisdom and deeper levels of joy, confidence and inner peace.

STRESS PREVENTION

Because disappointments are a normal part of life, it is best to develop positive responses to them. Here are some coping strategies:

Unwind. Find stress-relief techniques that fit your life and schedule. Soaking in a hot fragrant bath, listening to soothing music or simply taking a long walk will calm you.

Get in the spirit. Be faithful to a spiritual practice. Make time to pray or to simply sit quietly and listen—inwardly. Make unwinding an essential and nonnegotiable part of your everyday life. Learn meditation.

Exercise. Researchers aren't sure how exercise beats stress, but they know that it positively affects our hormonal balance, producing serotonin, which greatly helps to reduce worry and stress. Any type of regular rigorous exercise or rhythmic movement works.

Breathe deeply. Some doctors recommend deep breathing for people who are anxious all the time. Close your eyes. Inhale deeply for four counts; then exhale for four counts and feel the peace—relax.

Reach out. Loneliness increases worry. Make dates with friends; read to your children; go to a social gathering. The more connected you are to your family, friends and community, the better you'll feel.

Stressed? Stretch!

A.

B.

C.

These simple, blissfully relaxing yoga stretches and poses will rejuvenate body and soul and ensure that the madness won't work your nerves.

A. **Intoxicating Bliss Pose.** Kneel with thighs and feet together and slowly sit back on your heels. Separate your feet and lower your buttocks between your heels. If this is too difficult, put a folded blanket or a bolster under your butt. Place your palms along the length of your foot. If you're uncomfortable, place a telephone book or a block on either side of your feet and rest your palms on them. Lift your torso, close your eyes and take deep, relaxing breaths. Hold for three to five minutes. This pose is not recommended for those with knee problems.

B. **Intense Chest Stretch.** Stand straight and relax your neck and shoulders. Inhaling, raise arms overhead and then exhale while rotating arms behind and bending elbows, clasping one elbow in each hand. Separate your legs about four feet apart. Next, inhale and look up, lifting your chest and elongating the spine. Then exhale while bending forward, rotating the pelvis so you don't strain your back. With your head down and eyes open, take one to three deep inhalations. Hold for 30 seconds to one minute.

C. Slowly straighten up, keeping your arms behind your back. Pivot your right foot 90 degrees to the right and your left foot just slightly less than that, making sure your torso and hips also turn to the right. Keeping your weight on your left leg, inhale and look up, and then exhale, slowly bending forward over your right leg. Hold for one to three deep breaths. Inhale, lift up your chest to 90 degrees, and pivot your feet to center. Exhale, and pivot left foot 90 degrees and right foot slightly less than that. Repeat pose on the opposite side. People with hypertension or a herniated disk should not perform this pose.

D. **Inverted Lake Pose.** This position is said to help regulate blood pressure, alleviate stress-related headaches and reduce depression. Place a firm bolster (or two bed pillows rolled tightly in a bath towel) against the wall. Lie on your left side with your hip on the bolster and your buttocks touching the wall. Swing both legs up against the wall and roll onto your back. Relax your spine, press

D.

E.

your shoulders to the floor, and open your arms to the side. Hold for three to ten minutes. For added relaxation, use a scented eye pillow. To end the pose, bend your knees, simultaneously rolling your legs and shoulders to the left, and slowly sit up. Refrain from doing this pose during menstruation.

E. **Downward-Facing Dog.** Place two blocks or telephone books shoulder width apart on a non-slip yoga mat or against a wall. Kneel and place your palms flat on the blocks. Tuck in your toes and inhale, lifting your tailbone toward the ceiling as you elongate your spine. Exhale, widening your shoulders and relaxing your head between your stretched arms. Hold for 30 to 60 seconds. This pose should not be done by people with hypertension or varicose veins, those who suffer from frequent headaches or women in the final stages of pregnancy.

MENTAL HEALTH WATCH: HEALING AFTER TRAUMA

If you or a loved one experiences a personal tragedy, know that grief and mourning are a natural and important part of the healing process. Here's how to help the light shine again:

- Allow yourself to feel. Cry, holler, beat your pillow if the spirit moves you. Feeling deeply helps you release the pain.
- Treat yourself very well. Take time off for the minivacation you've been postponing. At home, do what you know soothes you: Get a massage or a facial; take long aromatic baths.
- Normalize your life; return to the activities you enjoy.
- Avoid alcohol and caffeine.
- Stay close to people you know and love. Reach out to people you know care about you.

If feelings of sadness and loss continue for months or you have difficulty coping, visit a therapist or grief counselor.

OVERCOMING

"*Every one of us has power — define your power, and work it.*"

— JILL SCOTT

HOLDING
THE REINS

OPRAH WINFREY

Oprah Winfrey's blend of wisdom and insight is dispensed daily on her talk show, which has been number one since her 1986 national debut. In 2000, her magazine, O, The Oprah Magazine, had the most successful launch in publishing history. The winner of 37 Emmy Awards, she is an Oscar-nominated actress, a philanthropist, a book lover and a businesswoman extraordinaire—our first Black woman billionaire. Oprah has done so much to help so many find a place of wholeness within themselves.

Breaking the cycle:

"I remember seeing my grandmother hanging clothes on the line in her backyard in Mississippi. She said, 'Watch me, 'cause you'll be doing this one day.' I thought to myself, *No, I won't.* I just knew that was not going to be my future."

Beating the odds:

"For a culture of people who have been for so many years denied and deprived and lacking in self-esteem, it's very hard to see the possibilities in your future. It's hard because the world has told you—and given you ideas about—who you can be."

Career beginnings:

"Before my local Chicago show went national, the general manager said to me, 'You know you can't beat Phil Donahue [at the time the nation's number one talk-show host], so just go on the air and be yourself.' The night before I launched the national show I wrote in my journal, 'I wonder how it will change my life and what does all of this really mean? Maybe it means I have more to say.'"

Figuring it all out:

"I feel tremendously powerful because I have reached a point in life where my personality is aligned with what my soul came to do. I believe you have to use your ego for a higher good."

Life's mission:

"The single greatest moment in my life was giving gifts to children at a South African orphanage. When they opened their gifts, the joy was palpable. That moment I realized this is why I have the fame and the money and all the attention—to become a voice for these children. They will become my life's mission."

Winfrey's wisdom:

"It takes a lot of courage to be who you really are. Don't let the rest of the world tell you what that is."

49

ALICE SPRAGGINS

In 1908, the year Alice Spraggins was born, Teddy Roosevelt was in the White House, the Ford Model T had just been unveiled, and the NAACP didn't even exist. In her lifetime, Spraggins, a retired elementary-school teacher, has seen incredible changes and done extraordinary things. The Silver Spring, Maryland, resident has dined with presidents and traveled around the world—she has lived.

On longevity:

"When people ask what I've done to live so long, I say that in addition to my family's genes, it's been taking good care of myself. My 63-year-old daughter and her friends tell me, 'When I grow up, I want to be just like you.'"

Day by day:

"Walking around my house is exercise, and I piddle around the house all day to keep me active and busy and so I don't focus on my husband's being gone. Instead, I rearrange furniture, cook, dust and do the laundry. And I love to watch basketball. My favorite team is the Washington Wizards. I am still active with the Links; I've been a member for 53 years."

Playful pleasure:

"Playing cards can be relaxing. Poker is my favorite game. In my little group we don't play for much money, because we are all retired. I don't always win, although my friends say I do. I also play bridge. I used to tell my husband that when we are playing cards, we don't have time to gossip."

Wanderlust:

"I love to travel. In my earlier days I went to Europe and Hawaii—and I love a cruise. My husband worked with Presidents Kennedy and Johnson as deputy director of voter registration, so we traveled for his work quite a bit."

Lost love:

"I was married for 65 years when my husband died in April 2000. I cannot begin to tell you how much I miss my husband. Living that long with someone, he becomes a part of you."

What I know for sure:

"I'm blessed to feel well. I take no medication, and I'm enjoying life."

Spraggins's wisdom:

"Physical love doesn't last forever, but like outlasts love. If you like somebody, the relationship will go on forever."

90

NAOMI CAMPBELL

For more than a decade, London-born supermodel Naomi Campbell has been active in charities, among them the Red Cross Somalia Relief Fund and UNESCO, an organization for which she helped raise funds to build kindergartens throughout the world for poor children. Having shed her "bad girl" image, Campbell is finding solace in growing, learning and loving the resilient woman she's becoming.

Black beauty:

"Brown skin is beautiful. When I started modeling, I was told that I would never be on the cover of *Vogue*—but I have been. I'm very proud of being a Black woman and having been a symbol of victory for all Black women."

Finding herself:

"I'm trying to get out of the pattern of always trying to please people. I have matured, and I've learned to say, 'Sorry, I can't do it.' My behavior had to do with not feeling secure. When you're living in chaos, you keep living wrong. When I faced the facts, all things came together. I'm so much happier with myself than when I was younger."

Mother's love:

"I've never met my real father. Since I was a baby, my mom has been alone, taking care of everything, working hard. I always felt her independence. I have so much respect and admiration for her. If I do something she doesn't like, she'll let me know. She keeps me grounded. I need that honesty because of all the 'yes' people I encounter in this world."

Past mistakes:

"Growing up in front of the press, I've made mistakes. I have to control my reactions. And I've had disappointments with people who've used me. Now when I get disappointed, I move on."

Overcoming addictions:

"Today I don't drink or take anything that alters my natural consciousness. Recovery is the best thing that's ever happened to me, and I wish it could be taught to kids in schools. Once you know the recovery tools from 12-step programs, you never forget them. No one should be ashamed of going to 12-step meetings. It's healthy, and it's therapeutic."

Campbell's wisdom:

"When you get things right within yourself, you start to manifest it in your aura—you begin to understand life from deep within."

33

HOLDING THE REINS

19

JULIET GIRARD

Instead of chilling with friends, Juliet Girard spent the summer of 2002 trying to end world hunger. She and classmate Roshan Prabhu interned at Cornell University in the NASA SHARP Plus Program. Their project was to identify genes in rice plants that speed up the rate at which the plants flower. For their efforts, the pair won the prestigious Siemens Westinghouse competition and split the $100,000 grand prize. Also, while attending high school in Jersey City, Girard was on the soccer team and in the drama club, and she edited the school newspaper. One of eight children, Girard now attends Harvard University.

Motivating factors:

"A woman who directed the lab we worked in had seen people starving in Argentina. Farmers depended on certain crops, and they didn't have a lifeline if things didn't work out. That helped motivate us to wake up at 6:00 A.M. to go to the greenhouse, which is 110 degrees on a summer day, where we were bitten by bugs and covered in pollen. We knew we were working toward something more important than ourselves."

Awakenings:

"The summer project opened a whole new world of science for me. It was an amazing feeling to be able to say I helped do something for other people, and to see the result. It made my dream of being a scientist more solid."

Winning Westinghouse:

"People in my school had been in the competition and had never gotten very far. For three months straight we worked hard and did our best, and when we made it to the national finals, we were ecstatic. It was a superpositive experience being the first African-American to earn this honor. And it feels good to know that I have $50,000 in the bank for college."

Eight is enough:

"My parents both work full-time, so I help my little brother and sister with their homework and get them to bed. Coming from a big family, I've grown up with a sense of responsibility and a strong work ethic."

Girard's wisdom:

"Don't let anyone tell you that you're not as good as anyone else. Feel confident in what you do and just do it."

FRANKIE STEWART

Frankie Stewart retired after working for 30 years, and now she's busier than ever. She helps her husband in an Internet marketing company, and she sits on the board of several organizations. Crowned Ms. Senior America in 1996, she says her dream is to build a retreat for seniors. Twice married, Stewart, a cancer survivor, is also writing a book about dating after 60.

Philosophy:

"I have decided that I am going to live until I die and be my best every day. And it is important for my family to know how much I love them. You can't tell them you love them after you are gone, so I tell them and show them each day."

Life's lesson:

"When I was younger, I thought I had to be all things to all people and to put myself last. What I have learned is that you have to nurture yourself first, you have to be emotionally cared for, and then you can deal with other people. I have also learned that it's okay to say no."

Love lesson I:

"In my first marriage I waited on my husband hand and foot. In my second marriage I do things for my husband, but he does a lot for me. I ask for what I need, stand up for myself and say what I feel."

Turning point:

"My first husband was a womanizer. After 39 years of marriage, I realized it was a toxic situation, and I had to get out. He was shocked. It was rough financially, but it was an epiphany for me."

Love lesson II:

"I am in love with my husband of five years. We have a healthy relationship. He is a retired colonel and is used to calling the shots—and so am I. We understand that we can both call the shots."

Stewart's wisdom:

"Have a sense of purpose, and take responsibility for the choices you make. Be truthful to yourself and examine yourself.

69

MAN

Iman's modeling career was launched in the 1970's, when she was discovered by a photographer while a political science student at Nairobi University in Kenya. During her career the Somalian native became an inspiration for Black women to challenge and change the prevailing notions of beauty. Iman, who's married to rock star David Bowie, speaks five languages, runs two successful beauty companies, has published an autobiography and is actively involved in charities benefiting children. The mother of two daughters, Zuleka, 25, and Alexandria, 3, Iman keeps amazingly fit.

Staying fit:

"I get bored with fitness regimens, so I like to mix it up: I box, swim, jog and do a bit of yoga. In my family we're healthy eaters—not too much fat and lots of vegetables and fruit—so it has come to me naturally. I never diet, and I don't deprive myself of anything. All in moderation!"

Jumping into the ring:

"I put on 50 pounds during my last pregnancy. Although I lost most of it, the last ten pounds were the hardest. So I took up boxing, which not only got rid of the ten pounds but also made me a fan. Now I box three times a week."

Giving back:

"I have been raised to give to others, to live a life of service and to have a balance in my life. I have chosen children's charities that I am proud to be a part of: the Children's Defense Fund, Batoto Yetu and For All Kids Foundation."

Making time for self:

"I like gardening and visiting museums and galleries. Lately my little daughter has discovered the joy of African dance and drumming. Through her I discovered that it is pure joy! Spirituality is part of my everyday existence. My religion, Islam, is a cornerstone to my life—giving service and gratitude."

Iman's wisdom:

"Be the change that you want to see."

47

43

EVELYN EVANS

It was in 1986 that 26-year-old Evelyn Evans lost her job and was about to lose custody of her two children. Depressed, she turned to her childhood passion, reading. Evans would curl up for hours with an engrossing book. One day she received a gift from a friend. The gift, a book titled The Game of Life and How to Play It *by Florence Scovel Shinn, changed her life. Evans studied the principles she learned in the book and began to apply them. Today the accomplished international photo editor and single mother tutors adult literacy students, travels to foreign locales — including a life-changing trip to Dubai in the Middle East—stays fabulously fit and finds spiritual solace in the Word.*

Day of peace:

"I was raised a Roman Catholic but converted to the Baptist faith because the Catholic doctrine was not motivating me to seek God for myself. I was 35 years old when I wept for the first time during a worship service, at the place I now call my church home. I am most at peace on Sunday afternoons—after I've gone to church, the house is clean, I've made a good home-cooked meal and I know where my teenage children are."

De-stress tests:

"As I've gotten older, I've learned to avoid situations that stress me out, such as overcommitting myself, running errands instead of sitting down to relax at mealtime, chauffeuring my children around instead of having them take public transportation and buying things on credit that I don't really need. Saying no has become my saving grace. I also take my mind off my problems by focusing on someone else's needs. That's why I've been a literacy volunteer for almost ten years."

Love tip:

"A loving relationship factors into my well-being. I'm grateful that I was open to dating younger men. I've been involved with a man for the past six years who is 11 years my junior, and I can honestly say it is the best relationship I've ever had. When someone paid me the compliment of not only looking good for my age, but also of having a youthful disposition, I attributed it to this younger man's important presence in my life."

Evans's wisdom:

"Good sisterfriends are invaluable. Make time for catching up with them."

ALICIA KEYS

Even as a child, Alicia Keys was well on her way to becoming a stellar musician. At 7, she began studying the Suzuki method of classical piano, and years later when she graduated from New York City's High School of Performing Arts, she was valedictorian of her class. At 20, she recorded her debut CD, Songs in A Minor, *which immediately put her in the superstar circle and won her an armful of awards, including five Grammys. The young virtuoso remains as driven as ever, writing, producing—and faithfully taking her piano lessons every week.*

Formal training:

"The piano is my baby. My mother, who's a singer, persuaded me to get classical training, and I fell in love with it. Learning classical music gave me the confidence to play in front of people. No matter what I felt—nerves, fear, excitement—I did it. And it helped me get over my inhibitions."

Early influence:

"I liked Biggie and Tupac, U2 and Nirvana, but in junior high school, it was all about Mary J. Blige. Mary was like my friends and me. Her vibe was the blueprint for my early songwriting. Then, when I was 13, I discovered Marvin Gaye, Curtis Mayfield and my all-time favorite, Donny Hathaway. I was enraptured by their honesty. That's when I realized that I didn't have to use somebody else's blueprint. I could use my own life and the things I've seen, and I can be truthful about it."

True to your art:

"There are wonderful artists out there who are searching within themselves, pushing themselves to be the best. Then there's another group who are not assuming the responsibility that I think is theirs. When I feel as if somebody has written a song out of passion, and this song represents the life that brought the person to that point, I feel its sincerity. But when someone is doing something just for the sake of the dollar or to exploit a niche, then it's phony."

Keys's wisdom:

"Set personal and professional goals. Know what you want to do, trust it, and do it!

23

HOLDING THE REINS

JILL SCOTT

Jill Scott was part of a stunning burst of young poets who came on the scene in Philadelphia in the late 1990's. Reciting poems, humming songs and rapping lyrics, they rocked the room and the city. Scott was exciting, on time and on a mission to be heard. She is a sassy, soulful sistergirl with an old-school spirit wrapped up with new-school flair. Now she's a musical force of nature whose time has come.

Spirit talk:

"My grandmother came from a different era, a different time, telling her story without saying any words. She would hum while she cooked and cleaned. But more important, she would hum and sing praises. To have someone with that kind of herstory be able to express herself with so much passion without words is a kind of wealth that you can't put any price on. Sometimes when I sing, I get close to that place of hers. Then I can go deep into the history of who we are as a people. That kind of way-down-deep-in-the-pelvic-bone singing is not singing—it's a spirit talk."

Enduring influences:

"When I started to study the music of the late Sarah Vaughan, I began to believe that she was in some way in touch with me. When you're an artist—a human being, really—you don't go anywhere when you die. Your spirit is still around. Some of today's artists are definitely being touched by people of the past."

Ripe with life:

"It's important to pick up the baton, but when it's time to pass it on, you do so. I've never held on to one thing for too long. I don't like to make one thing my life. There are more arenas to be explored. There may be some arenas that come before singer, before poet, before woman. It may be on different tiers that I don't know or quite understand yet, and I'm comfortable with that."

A love supreme:

"Being in a relationship, having a husband, knowing that I have his complete back and that he has mine as well—that is very powerful."

Scott's wisdom:

"Every one of us has power, and it's a matter of taking the time and defining what that power is and working it. It doesn't have to be on a large scale for great things to occur."

ANGELA BASSETT

Long before she became an accomplished actress, Angela Bassett was the dutiful oldest daughter of a hardworking single mother from St. Petersburg, Florida. Raised in the church, Bassett was expected to work hard and be dignified in all she did. That strength of character and sense of self come across in whatever role she plays.

Childhood trauma:

"My mother had a boyfriend who fondled my sister and me—scared the crap out of me. Fortunately, it didn't get past fondling. That was detrimental enough. And my mother believed me and banished him from her life. That strengthened me. Still, it couldn't help but inform the whole fabric of who I am sexually. I still don't like to be looked at in a certain way."

Family values:

"I sacrificed to wait and find the perfect husband. I wanted to do it decently and in order. I think I'll have a child whether or not it's from my own body. I'm holding out hope that it's going to happen for us."

Life's challenges:

"You've got to constantly keep yourself motivated and inspired. It helps to have good friends and family, who can be honest with you when you feel down."

Reel life:

"Our image on film travels all over the world. And an image of us killing one another, taking drugs, kicking our women in the behind or kicking one another in the head hurts. There's enough of that. Some people find that funny and call it art. But there has to be balance. Perhaps that's why I'm attracted to strong women who overcome or do amazing things."

Real life:

"We're always looking for something bigger, better. In the end I may have said no to some things I should've said yes to, but at the time I had good reasons. But I'm happy, and there's nothing else I'd rather be."

Bassett's wisdom:

"If it's going to be, then it will happen."

45

59

EVELYN BAKON

Evelyn Bakon has a full-time job as one of only a few software-application specialists at a major law firm, where she began as a legal secretary 27 years ago. She has co-owned a women's boutique in Boston, Massachusetts, for the past 22 years, and also has been an events planner for the past 11. In her spare time, Bakon thinks up adventures to have with her four sisters. Her sister, Ophelia, appears on page 50.

Opportunities seized:

"I started the business as a personal shopper in 1974 and it grew to have so many clients, in three years I was able to turn it into a retail boutique with three of my sisters. In the early 1990's a friend asked me to help put together a sorority dinner. Then others started asking for help planning functions, and the next thing I knew, we had started an events-planning business, doing weddings, dinners and teas."

Seeing the world, even solo:

"I've never been happier—or busier. A few years ago I had to travel to Switzerland alone, and recently I spent two weeks by myself in France on vacation. I discovered that when I travel alone, I'm more open to meeting and having wonderful conversations with great people. I have beautiful memories of those trips."

Spreading cheer:

"I'm a big smiler. And honey, that is why I look good now! People say to me, 'Thank you for your smile and your kindness.' Like everyone else I've had my problems, but I don't let them get me down."

Bakon's wisdom:

"Laugh, smile, and make yourself happy!"

33

QUEEN LATIFAH

Dana Owens, who renamed herself Queen Latifah, blazed a trail in rap when men still ruled the mic. More than a decade later, she remains center stage. But she's not serving up the same old stuff. The Grammy Award–winning musician continues to add new jewels to her crown. She has been a sitcom diva and a talk-show host. She's an entrepreneur and a recording-industry executive. Latifah not only received an Oscar nomination for her role in the feature film Chicago, *but she was also executive producer and star of* Bringing Down the House, *which opened at number one at the box office in 2003. She is also the cochairman of the Lancelot H. Owens Scholarship Foundation, established in memory of her brother.*

Spiritual boost:

"I have my faith in God. I receive peace from knowing I can put my life in His hands or ask for His help. Once you realize there is a higher power, you know that you're not alone and you have a purpose on the planet. You control your destiny. You seize it, take it and lead it, instead of letting the day lead you where it may."

Family first:

"My mom never changes. If everything else fails, I still have a home to go to, and I have a family who loves me a lot. I had my father for a part of my life, but I had enough love from my mother—and from my father before he split with her—so I was okay."

Know thyself:

"I am what I am, and that's that. If there's one thing I know, it's myself, so I don't need to even pretend I'm going to be like other people."

Latifah's wisdom:

"Everything comes down to your choices and decisions. Look inside yourself and trust you more than you trust anyone."

BECOME YOUR OWN DREAM WEAVER

Get still, close your eyes, and envision the kind of life you want. Be very specific: Picture yourself in perfect health, living in a dwelling that reflects your tastes, busily pursuing the kind of work that inspires you, and taking on other pursuits that will become threads in the personal tapestry, the legacy, you leave behind. And always think of the blessings you'd like to pass on to your loved ones: values, wisdom, heirlooms, property, money. Whatever your contributions are, they will have an impact on many long after you're gone. Be the architect of your dreams: Build them—one meaningful step at a time.

DREAM A BETTER LIFE

We want to prosper and live life abundantly, but not at the expense of inner peace and balance. We want a life that's about more than just what we can acquire. Here Susan L. Taylor shares some strategies for creating a way of living that will help keep you happy, healthy and successful all the days of your life.

Eliminate anything that is not nourishing, nurturing or life-sustaining. We can't give from a dry well. Self-care isn't selfish; it's the smartest thing we can do. When we don't take care of ourselves, we can't care for our own. What's good for us is good for our family, our community, our world.

Take quiet time to think about how you want to live now and in the future. Write down and commit to memory your core values and the principles that will keep you fit and focused and guide and govern your life. Then when the daily dramas threaten to rob you of your serenity and focus, remember what you're choosing for yourself.

Remember this truth: We were born to succeed, and there really are no negatives, no mistakes—only lessons on living in the light.

Don't doubt your abilities or forget your place—standing on the threshold of the future our ancestors lived and died for. With every breath, surrender your fears to faith. Help God help you: Why stand under Niagara Falls with a thimble? Have a bucket in your hands.

See your work as a sacred task. Whether we are running a company or cleaning toilets, we must remember that through our work we serve God and one another. Our work is a channel through which we can contribute to the community, to society. The most menial task should be done with dignity and pride. Think of your work as an opportunity to love and serve joyfully.

Remember that you are bigger than you've been taught to believe. We move through a miracle greater than we can imagine. We *are* success. We are life living and loving itself. The goal is to merge our inner and outer worlds—to bring the wisdom and harmony we discover within us into the world each day. God has prepared a place for us. We must be faithful in preparing ourselves to take that place.

Focus each day on those critical few things you must do. Don't stress yourself by overscheduling activities or underallocating time in which to do them. And don't forget to breathe.

Watch your mind and your mouth. Don't complain. Rather, focus on solutions. The gift of creative intelligence means you have the ability and responsibility to be proactive in shaping your world.

Be grateful. Strive to live each moment in gratitude for your life. A thankful heart helps to multiply your blessings.

LIVE YOUR JOY

Here is Iyanla Vanzant's wisdom about how we can all begin feeling more joyful and fulfilled—right now:

Ask for what you want, and believe you can have it. The hard times during your childhood may have given you the idea that you'll never be financially comfortable. It is time to disassociate yourself from such negative beliefs. Repeat: "I am blessed with the tools for success." Sing uplifting songs while paying bills.

Count your blessings—again. You are thankful for your mate, but what about those faraway good friends? When you find yourself focused on what you don't have, shift into gratitude. Say, "My friend is just a call or an E-mail away."

Be a better friend to yourself and others. Affirm your ability to meet challenges. Compliment yourself and those you admire. You bring more love into your life by being positive.

Drop any facade and be real. Honest communication and heartfelt caring result in true intimacy.

Practice acceptance of every challenge. Think and affirm aloud: "I can't wait to see the good growing out of this experience." In the meantime, be blessed.

133

"*When I go walking before dawn,*
I get to appreciate God's gifts."
— ROSALIND HALL

HEALTHY
LIVING

BEVERLY TAYLOR

For most of us, reaching retirement is a definitive benchmark, but not for Beverly Taylor. When she retired at 60 as an elementary-school principal, she began mentoring principals and became an adjunct college professor. In 2003, at the blossoming age of 68, however, Taylor declined a college teaching assignment so she could experience the thrill of visiting Africa for her first safari in Tanzania. Her youthful mother, Hilda Stephenson, appears on page 64.

Eating divinely:

"For breakfast I concoct a berry drink—blueberries, strawberries, raspberries and grapes—in a blender with rice milk. For lunch and dinner I eat fresh vegetables with protein, such as chicken or fish. It makes me feel less stuffed. Dark-green leafy vegetables are a mainstay in my daily diet. I am always chopping up onions and garlic for sautéing my veggies."

Staying fit as a fiddle:

"Five days a week, I exercise for one hour in the morning. I get up around 8:00 and start with stretching—including standing on my toes, which is excellent for my hamstring and calf muscles. Then I usually run in place and finish with abdominal exercises. When the weather is nice, I alternate running in place with outdoor racewalking, which is wonderful. You use every muscle in your body— and it prevents osteoporosis. Golf keeps my mind working, because I have to constantly think about my shots. I started playing at 60, and I love it as much as I did playing tennis and skiing for many years, but which I had to stop because of a torn cartilage in my knee."

Athletic accomplishment:

"When I was 60, I racewalked for 26.2 miles in the New York City Marathon, and I didn't care that everyone else was running. When I crossed that finish line, I felt such incredible exhilaration. Sure I was sore for a few days, but it was worth it."

Last big adventure:

"Visiting the Serengeti Reservation in Tanzania was among the most poignant experiences in my life. There is nothing like the beauty of nature. The scenery was breathtaking—and to see the animals in their natural habitat was most incredible."

Taylor's wisdom:

"We are mind, body and spirit—so we must nourish all three until we die."

68

HELEN HEMMINGS

For retired nurse Helen Hemmings, turning 86 meant stepping up her exercise program, volunteering at the New York City senior center where she resides, as well as increasing her computer activities and spending more time with her daughter and grandchildren. For the vivacious Hemmings, walking and meditation are the keys to a more peaceful life. Her daughter, Beverly, appears on page 150.

Brainpower:

"I like the computer and spend at least an hour a day surfing the Web and soaking up information on the latest trends in health programs. Keeping your brain stimulated is essential. I also read the newspaper every morning while eating breakfast."

Staying healthy:

"I exercise four to six days each week. I use the treadmill, do free weights and use the exercise ball, which is a lot of fun. When I turned 76, I started developing arthritis, so exercising has become crucial. Although I am not a swimmer, water exercises really alleviate the symptoms. I allow myself one cup of coffee daily, and I eat oatmeal to keep my blood pressure down. On weekends I give myself a treat, like a blueberry muffin or a bagel."

Making time for meditation:

"I was very tense for much of my life, and I did not appreciate nature—birds, butterflies, the beautiful sky above. Thanks to the relaxation techniques I've learned at annual spa retreats, I can live in the moment, be quiet and focus on what's going on inside. Now I try to meditate two to three times a week at home. I close my eyes and focus on one word I love—or on the *ohmmmm* sound, which supposedly creates the best vibration."

Dance fever:

"I love dancing, but because there aren't enough males in my retirement home, I don't get to indulge my passion for ballroom dancing. Instead, I do line dancing."

Hemmings's wisdom:

"You have to ask yourself, *What can I do for others?* In the end you are really giving to yourself."

86

BEVERLY JOHNSON

In 1974, at age 22, Beverly Johnson made history as the first African-American woman to grace the cover of Vogue. *With that, the Buffalo-born former teen swimming coach became a supermodel—appearing on more than five hundred major magazine covers during her 20-year modeling career. Today her licensing deal has garnered among the highest direct-mail wig sales, and her jewelry collection debuted in stores in 2003. Several years ago, a medical crisis forced her to take charge of her health.*

Female crisis:

"In my thirties I was diagnosed with fibroids—benign tumors in my uterus. When I was 45, they had grown so large I had to have a myomectomy, surgery to remove fibroids. Later the doctor told me he needed to remove one of my ovaries. I had signed a release, but I didn't understand what it meant."

Surgical setback:

"After the first surgery, I had excruciating pain, and I was menstruating every day for one year, which resulted in anemia. When the fibroids grew back, two doctors recommended a hysterectomy. I was ready for a solution to my misery, but again, I didn't understand the specifics. After the second surgery, I was rushed back for another operation. I was bleeding internally and nearly went into cardiac arrest. A few weeks later, doubled over in pain, I was rushed into surgery again for a hernia near the hysterectomy incision."

Finding balance:

"Suddenly I began having night sweats. I had signed another release before the surgery that allowed them to remove my other ovary, but I didn't fully understand that it would lead to immediate menopause. My doctor prescribed hormones—estrogen and testosterone—but it took nearly two years to get the right balance. Meanwhile, I was depressed, irritable and crying a lot. I wasn't interested in sex—a first for me."

Moving forward:

"Now I play golf six days a week, and I work with a trainer to strengthen muscle groups. I've always eaten healthily, but I had to add estrogen-rich foods to my diet. I use soy products to replace dairy, and I take coral calcium supplements for osteoporosis prevention. I am in the best shape I've ever been in."

Johnson's wisdom:

"It's our responsibility as women to be in the driver's seat when it comes to our health. We have to educate ourselves—and not be shy or passive."

51

77

BETTY GRICE

*After decades as a public-school teacher, Betty Grice became
frustrated and said good-bye to the school system. Then, through
work at local community centers, she found a new career as a fitness
instructor. This grandmother teaches swimming, yoga and aerobics
to seniors and teenagers.*

Building mind and body:

"Exercise is good for me mentally and physically. It helps keep
me patient. I find that things bother me more when I miss my
classes. Working with children and adults is good for everyone—
adults learn patience, and children learn to have more respect for
their elders."

Eating for pleasure:

"In the mornings I drink lemon and water at room temperature to
get me started. My favorite munchies are grapes and raw carrots.
The less meat I eat, the better I feel. I crave lemon meringue pie,
Jell-O pudding and carrot cake, but only indulge once a week."

Embracing age:

"I never thought I would live this long! That's why I constantly
stop and think, *Is there something I'm supposed to do that I have not
done yet?*"

Regimen for a healthy soul:

"Music inspires and relaxes me. Sometimes when I get blue or
lonely, I put on my jazz tapes and I feel great. I am also at peace
whenever I am around birds, the sky and greenery, where it is
quiet. I even like the sound of the crickets."

Grice's wisdom:

"You have to like yourself and keep on pushing, and after a while
you find that you do what's good for you naturally."

ROSALIND HALL

*Rosalind Hall, who owns a fitness studio in Stuart, Florida, always
has been hardworking and flexible. Over the years, Hall has worked as
a meatpacker, a telephone company employee and a leotard designer.
In 1992 she started working in a gym, began exercising and eventually
became a certified fitness instructor. That inspired her to convert
part of her home into a studio, which now is thriving with more than
60 clients.*

Fitness routine and goals:

"I do cardiovascular walking and jogging and weight training several
times a week. Working out makes me feel strong. I'm also doing
some nontraditional fitness training, such as mountain climbing and
mountain biking."

Studio goal:

"Right now my next goal is to build an obstacle course. I'd like to
have a little boot camp."

Her God connection:

"When I get up to go walking before dawn, I get to appreciate
God's gifts, the stars and the moon. I look out at the water and
see the dolphins and watch the sunset—every single day. When
you're outside in nature, it's very apparent what life's all about.
It's about gratitude—giving thanks."

Health hint:

"Women are good at dealing with pain and accepting it—instead
of taking care of it. If something is bothering me, I do something
about it. I don't let it linger and think that it will go away."

Quick cool-outs:

"I need to have a hug. Hugging is a good de-stressor, and so are
movies. But nothing sad, of course."

Hall's wisdom:

"You have to be comfortable in your skin."

50

VELMA JOHNSON

When Velma Johnson finally found her niche, she'd already been a nurse's aide, a clerk typist and a housewife. Answering her soul's true calling at age 42, Johnson opened her own fashion boutique, which she successfully ran for 25 years. Currently, she is doing research for a Black historical fashion exhibition. She's also installing a greenhouse in the kitchen of her Brooklyn brownstone.

Wake-up call:

"After menopause, I had a general malaise, and I didn't have any energy. I went on estrogen replacement therapy, but I didn't like the idea of what it was doing to my body, so I stopped. I began looking into herbs and natural remedies, like wild yam and don quai, which helps relieve the discomfort and hot flashes."

Finding a cure:

"I went to many doctors over the years to treat my osteoarthritis and a pinched nerve. Nothing helped. Then I tried tai chi, and within three days I had no more pain."

Her workout routine:

"I've been doing tai chi each morning for three years. Most of us don't breathe from the proper source. In tai chi, we breathe from our navel. We call it cellular breathing. It boosts my energy. I also take walks at night at a moderate pace."

Health regimen:

"I have a tendency toward high blood pressure, so I take a lot of vitamins and herbs, including garlic pills, vitamins E, C and B complexes, and calcium. I also get colonics, and I do a one-day fast once a month, when I drink water as well as blend up fruits and vegetables to drink all day."

Her little extras:

"I designed a bathroom spa, and once a week I light candles and take a bubble bath with Epsom salts in it. I give myself a facial scrub and a pedicure, and I massage myself with a dry brush to energize my body. It's pampering for me, and it feels good!"

Johnson's wisdom:

"In working on yourself, you get in touch with a higher power in your life, who is really in charge. You find out it's not about you. Once you come to grips with that, life is not a struggle. I leave everything up to the higher power. Most things aren't that important."

73

$\mathcal{Y}$VONNE BONITTO DOGGETT

During her 20 years as an economic-development executive, Yvonne Doggett has had an impact on Atlantic City's thriving casino business by being involved in the start-up of Bally's casino. Meanwhile, the wife, mother, grandmother and gourmet cook maintains a fitness program, plays golf and is an active member in community organizations.

Passion for sports:

"I used to play tennis, but now golf is my game. Instead of riding in a cart while golfing, I walk to get exercise. I go out by myself on spring evenings to get in 9 holes. It's my communion with God. The green fairway is so beautiful—it's a wonderful experience. I play 18 holes in the summer."

Dining divinely:

"I am a lifetime member of Weight Watchers. For breakfast and lunch, I eat high protein and low carbohydrate meals. For dinner, however, I have my 'rewards meals.' I eat and drink everything that I want within an hour—that includes one martini, an appetizer, salad, soup, and fish, chicken or beef. I love the taste of real butter, hollandaise and béarnaise sauces—artificial margarine and low-fat salad dressings simply won't do! I also belong to a gourmet club—we host dinners or dine at restaurants in different cities."

Loving and sharing:

"September 2003 was my husband and my fortieth anniversary. What makes our marriage work is the ability to give each other space—literally. We have two bedrooms and two separate bathrooms. I love to surround myself with scents, and my husband doesn't. I need quiet time for contemplation, writing and yoga."

Most valuable resource:

"I talk to God as if He is my roommate. I thank Him daily for my blessings."

Higher learning:

"Retirement is not part of my vocabulary. Life is about learning. As long as I have a career, I will continue to hone my skills and obtain additional ones so I can compete in the marketplace and mentor others. That is why I went back to graduate school for my master's degree at 56. Now I can lean back on the ladder to help others up."

Doggett's wisdom:

"Age is just a number. My spirit is eternally 18—that's how old I always feel."

BEVERLY HEMMINGS

At the onset of the new millennium, Beverly Hemmings, who was approaching her sixtieth year, made the commitment to put her youthful philosophies into practice. The superbly fit grandmother formed Youthful Aging, a motivational-speaking company, to educate individuals and corporations on aging gloriously. Hemmings and her 86-year-old mother, Helen, who appears on page 138, are living examples of ageless vitality.

Feeling fit:

"For me, yoga is a moving meditation—my limbs, muscles, spleen, heart and lungs are being worked. When I turned 61, I added Pilates to my exercise regime, incorporating a series of core-strengthening abdominal and spine exercises that I could do at home on a mat. The beauty of Pilates and yoga exercises is that it's never too late to begin."

Breath of life:

"Breathing deeply into your diaphragm sends fresh oxygen to the cells. I had to learn how to breathe after a life-transforming experience. In 1991, I developed a chronic cough. I had an X-ray, and the doctor discovered a mass, which he thought was cancer because of its size, shape and location. Further tests proved that there was no cancer, but that false alarm was a wake-up call of how precious life is."

Living single:

"I was married once in my early twenties for about three years, and I've been single ever since. Being single has been given a bad rap. When you learn to love yourself, you can enjoy life immensely—and relationships can be seen as ice cream on top of a delicious pie. In life, relationships come and go, and you can still be whole when they're long gone."

Hemmings's wisdom:

"To keep your brain active, always be curious. Just because we age doesn't mean we have to be dried up, stale and detached from life."

MIND YOUR BODY, NURTURE YOUR HEALTH

We all want to live long, healthy lives. We are talking about the kind of life that allows us to bound up a few flights of stairs without gasping for breath. Or sprint down the block to catch a bus effortlessly. Or hear a good joke without chronic coughing jags. Yes, there are great demands on our time, and to cope with our endless pressures, this is the smartest thing each of us must do: put our health at the center of our swirling schedules. Eating well, taking minibreaks throughout the day, regular exercise and medical checkups are more important than our most pressing tasks. Make maintaining wellness your top priority and you'll start to notice that your mind, body and soul are all working together to serve you—and every important thing in your life not only gets done but is done well.

EAT SMART

By making some smart and simple food choices, you can head off those extra pounds. Here are some tips on healthy eating strategies:

Eat breakfast. Studies have shown that people who eat high-fiber breakfasts are less likely to overeat at lunch.

Eat lots of fruit and vegetables. Adding colorful fruits as well as leafy green and cruciferous (broccoli, Brussels sprouts, cauliflower) vegetables to your plate can help fill you up and nourish you. They are rich in disease-fighting vitamins, antioxidants, potassium and folic acid. Make fruits and vegetables a diet staple in your household.

Make walking an after-dinner routine. This simple enjoyable ritual will help prevent digestive problems and weight gain. One of the worst things for our health is lying down after eating. Start a new routine by taking a walk after dinner.

Don't deprive yourself. Eat what you love and what is good for you. And plan your exercise ritual according to the amount of calories you've ingested. If you had a hunk of chocolate cake for dessert yesterday, you owe your body a slightly longer and more vigorous workout today. Remember this principle: The calories your body doesn't burn turn to fat.

PREVENTING HEART DISEASE

These important steps can save your life even if you are at high risk for heart disease. Here are critical measures to take—right now:

No butts about it. If you smoke, commit to quit today. Ask your physician about smoking-cessation programs and products.

Walk, run, jump! Commit to 30 minutes of moderate to vigorous physical exercise most days of the week. Make no excuses about why you don't work out, and start reaping the enormous benefit of exercise. Look into exercise programs at your local YWCA or gym or on video. You can also walk your way to fitness. The Nurses' Health Study—the longest major women's health survey ever conducted—showed that women who walked briskly for at least three hours a week reduced their risk of having a heart attack, the number one killer of all Americans, by 30 to 40 percent.

Eat a healthy diet. Consuming two or three servings of whole grains (from sources such as brown rice, oatmeal or whole wheat bread) each day can reduce your risk of heart attack by 27 percent, according to the Nurses' Health Study. Eating 25 grams of soy (approximately three glasses of soy milk) per day will benefit the heart as well. Also, eat at least five servings of vegetables and fruits daily and limit your fat and sodium.

Maintain your ideal body weight. If you're overweight, losing 10 to 15 pounds can reduce heart-disease risk. Forget crash diets—they don't work, promote greater weight gain and ruin your health. Eat less, develop healthy eating habits and exercise and you'll shed pounds gradually and permanently.

Keep count of your cholesterol. Get your cholesterol checked annually or more often if you have tested high. Your total cholesterol level should remain under 200 milligrams per deciliter (more than 40 mg/dl of HDL or "good" cholesterol; less than 100 mg/dl of LDL, or "bad" cholesterol).

Watch your blood pressure. If your blood pressure is normal, have it checked during visits to your doctor. If it's too high, or if you have a family history of high blood pressure, ask your doctor how often you need to have it checked.

Get regular checkups with a doctor who is sensitive to your needs. Choose physicians who take risk factors seriously. Don't let a doctor dismiss symptoms like chest pains, extreme fatigue or shortness of breath.

Get treatment for high blood pressure. If eating a healthy diet and exercising don't work, your doctor may prescribe medicine to help reduce the risk of heart attack or to improve heart functions, including antiplatelet and anticoagulant drugs, beta-blockers and ACE inhibitors.

Drink alcohol sparingly—or not at all. Too much alcohol can raise blood pressure and certain fat levels in the blood.

THE ULTIMATE ENERGY DRINK

Contrary to common belief, water—not caffeinated drinks—is the best beverage for boosting energy. That's because water keeps the body's blood volume up, ensuring that ample amounts of nutrients and oxygen get transported to the cells. Water also helps the body digest and make use of vitamins that are critical for maintaining stamina. And it's water that enables crucial electrical messages—those that make your muscles move—to travel between cells.

Water: The Elixir of Life

Health experts agree that many of the maladies that ruin lives could have been avoided by drinking adequate amounts of water. So drink up!

- Have eight to twelve cups of water a day.
- Drink at least two cups of water two to two and a half hours before working out, then two cups about 15 minutes before your activity.
- During exercise, down about a half cup every 15 minutes.
- Drink at least two cups after your workout, more if you've exercised for more than an hour.

155

PHOTOGRAPHY CREDITS

Front Cover
Queen Latifah: Robert Deutschman
Jill Scott: Marc Baptiste
Bernie Mac: Jonathan Mannion
T.D. Jakes: Courtesy of The Potter's House
*   Ministries*
Jacqueline Peters Cannon: Carlo Dalla Chiesa

Table of Contents
Page 6: Spicer

Introduction
Page 9: Spicer

Living in Love
Page 10: Spicer
13–15: Cliff Watts
16: Danielle and Shay Meir Peretz
19: Robert Deutschman
21: Spicer
22: Carlo Dalla Chiesa
25: Jonathan Mannion
27: Matthew Jordan Smith
28: Frits Berends
31: Matthew Jordan Smith

Keeping the Faith
Page 32: Spicer
35: Carlo Dalla Chiesa
36: Sante D'Orazio
39–41: Spicer
42: Carlo Dalla Chiesa
45–46: Anthony Mandler, Courtesy of J Records
47: Robert Deutschman
49: Courtesy of The Potter's House Ministries
51: Keith Major
52: Luciana Pampalone
55: Corbis
56: Courtesy of Amelia Island Plantation
57: Fabrice Trombert

Shaping Up
Page 58: Matthew Jordan Smith
61: Paul Lange
63: Robert Deutschman
65: Matthew Jordan Smith
67: Kwaku Alston
68: Matthew Jordan Smith

71: Kwaku Alston
72–75: David Morgan

Overcoming
Page 76: Kwaku Alston
78–81: Carlo Dalla Chiesa
83: Paul Lange
85: Keith Major, Courtesy of Curtis Martin
86: Luciana Pampalone
89: Warrick Saint, Courtesy of J Records
91: Kwaku Alston
93: Paul Lange
95: Matthew Jordan Smith
97: Fabrice Trombert
98–99: Adam Olszewski

Holding the Reins
Page 100: Marc Baptiste
102: Fabrizio Ferri, Courtesy of Harpo
*   Productions, Inc.*
105: Kwaku Alston
107–109: Norman Jean Roy
110: Peter Chin
113: Keith Major
115: Courtesy of Iman
116: Paul Lange
119–121: Spicer
122: Marc Baptiste
125: Carlo Dalla Chiesa
126: Kwaku Alston
128: Robert Deutschman
130: Daniela Federici
132: Kwaku Alston
133: Robert Deutschman

Healthy Living
Page 154: Carlo Dalla Chiesa
137: Matthew Jordan Smith
139: Carlo Dalla Chiesa
141: Fadil Berisha
143: Keith Major
145: Carlo Dalla Chiesa
147: Paul Lange
149: Matthew Jordan Smith
150: Carlo Dalla Chiesa
152: Gary Buss, Getty Images
155: Nick Clement, Getty Images

*I*NDEX